Damage Control

Damage Control

Women on the Therapists, Beauticians, and Trainers Who Navigate Their Bodies

Edited by Emma Forrest

AVON

An Imprint of HarperCollins*Publishers*

HarperCollins books may be purchased for educational, business, or sales promotional use. For information please write: Special Markets Department, HarperCollins Publishers, 10 East 53rd Street, New York, NY 10022.

An extension of this copyright page appears on pages 281–282.

FIRST EDITION

Designed by Elizabeth M. Glover

Library of Congress Cataloging-in-Publication Data

Damage control : women on the therapists, beautitians, and trainers who navigate their bodies / edited by Emma Forrest. — 1st ed.
      p.   cm.
ISBN: 978–0–06–117535–0
ISBN–10: 0–06–117535–8
1. American literature—Women authors. 2. American literature—21st century.
3. Women—Literary collections.   I. Forrest, Emma.

PS508.W7D36 2007
820.8'09287—dc22   2006037865

07 08 09 10 11   ID/RRD   10 9 8 7 6 5 4 3 2

For Toni Napier

Contents

Part V: WAX POETIC

Damage Control

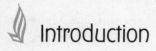 # Introduction

In the pilot episode of *Nip/Tuck*, Sean yells at his brilliant ex–med student wife: "You shop, you lunch, you get your vagina waxed like a porn star." It has, of course, crossed my mind that all this post-feminist primping is no more than a form of procrastination. The more we can achieve, the more body parts we find to "maintain." "I'm sure that somewhere in a laboratory in Switzerland a clever scientist is this very moment dreaming up a cream," writes Julie Burchill, "to be used on the inside of the elbow." The mystery makeup artist in Part III is less cynical: "Sometimes," she says, "the only peace in a woman's day is the twenty minutes when she's getting her toes done, or her fingernails done. The only time she has when someone else is completely focusing on her. One of those rare opportunities when someone's looking her in the eyes, and seeing what she needs."

That's what this collection is about: the intimate strangers who work with the surface and get to the depths. If women tell their secrets to their hairdressers, what might they share upside down on a masseuse's table, or hand in hand with a manicurist? And what do you tell the aesthetician when she doesn't just see your scalp, she sees your *vagina*? In HD detail. Lying on the waxing table, I always have to stop myself from grabbing Rada by the lapels and crying, "Do our genitals haunt your nightmares?" So I was glad to have not only excellent essays by such a talented array of novelists, journalists, poets, actresses, and comedians, but also interviews with the "intimates" themselves: waxers, hairdressers, facialists, chiropractors, and the above-quoted woman who is the in-house makeup artist at one of the country's biggest strip clubs. Who knew?

I am delighted to say this collection is full of "who knew?" You could start on page 250 where Maysan Haydar takes us into the world of Arab beauty rituals: veiled women beautified by and for other veiled women. Or start with Rachel Resnick's travelogue as mystery, in which she gets a New Year's Eve massage in Mexico, traversing her darkest holiday memory as a legendary masseuse traverses her body.

It is a particular pleasure to have in this collection Jennifer Belle, perhaps my favorite American novelist. Here she writes about a spa certificate that led to an unexpected visit from the past.

Rose McGowan's thoughts on beautician etiquette are as precise and funny as the actress herself. Susie Essman you know as the perpetually enraged Susie Greene of *Curb Your*

Enthusiasm. It's fascinating to see her anger aimed at the way religion has curtailed female beauty (read empowerment) rituals.

To those who feared this collection might carry with it an air of *Upstairs, Downstairs* or us and them, Marian Keyes's "Hair Rage" hilariously captures the intense intimidation factor that can come with a salon visit. In "By a Hair," Samantha Dunn points out that a woman's finances are still a taboo topic of discussion and shows just how far a girl who can't pay rent will go to keep her color.

Minnie Driver has long been celebrated for her unique beauty. In her first published essay, she writes about the kindly French hairdresser who tried to help the fourteen-year-old Minnie see what she would one day become as she waddles, ugly duckling to her sister's swan, through a miserable family holiday.

The British-Nigerian Helen Oyeyemi, whose debut novel last year—*The Icarus Girl*—must have made her the most critically lauded teenager in *New York Book Review* history, writes about black hair in an Enid Blyton culture. It is one of five essays about hair, and I think that's because, as Maggie Paley explains in her charming essay "Felix Gets a Haircut" (comparing her grooming regimen to her cat's), hair is always with us.

Sarah Jones, who won a Tony last year for her one-woman show *Bridge and Tunnel*, is a great heroine of mine. I went for a pedicure with her and felt tremendous relief that someone who does as much good in the world also likes having her toes painted. Her poem "a wax poetic" questions how she and her waxer both got there. She is the essence of modern feminism. As the cofounder of *Bust* magazine, Marcelle Karp knows a lot about this. "Tender" chronicles her attempt to be a tough chick while in physical and emotional agony.

Sarah Bennett is uneasy with the bikini wax craze, so much so that it ends a friendship. Making her debut as an essayist here, Bennett demonstrates a rare gift, funny and true, for capturing the interior emotional life of young women. Speaking of, Barbara Hall brought strong, left-of-center female voices to television as the creator of *Judging Amy* and *Joan of Arcadia*. She writes of finding her own voice in "Let Me Take You Down."

I had told my contributors that their essays need not be positive about their "intimate"; still, I was stunned by Francesca Lia Block's "Not a Pretty Story," in which she recounts her entanglement with an unsavory plastic surgeon, and Laren Stover's "The Chi Gong Show," in which she traces the $10K she spent in one year under the spell of a chi gong master who said he could cure her breast cancer.

As you will read, Ellen Karsh abhors being touched and is proud to admit it. What does it say that the other three don't-touch-me's—Julie Burchill, Suzanne Moore and Barbara Ellen—are all British? Julie imagines a dystopian future, where women are relaxing in scented baths whilst men download barnyard porn. Suzanne gets blacklisted by a homeopath. And Barbara picks a fight with her personal trainer.

Lena Levin's essay covers hair, pedicure, and massage and asks, "If you can't speak up for yourself in the beauty salon, can you do it in real life?" Lena Levin is a pseudonym, and even I don't know who she is. All I can say is how happy I was when I received her extraordinary essay.

My own essay, "A Fixed Ideal," investigates an old obsession with a Buddhist tattoo artist. Many consider tattoo terribly ugly and can't imagine what place it holds in a beauty book. My reply is that, as far as I'm concerned, like the hypothetical place where communism meets fascism, ugly and beautiful have more in common than they know.

Last but not least, it makes me incredibly proud to publish my own mother, Judy Forrest, whose *Vogue* interviews with people like Terry Gilliam and Fay Weldon first interested me in writing. I always knew I loved New York in the fifties and sixties, but it took reading her story to realize I had been having false memory syndrome: hers.

When my mum first came over to L.A. to meet my boyfriend's mom, I took them to Jessica Nail Clinic on Sunset, which is where I got the idea for this book. Full of Old Hollywood matriarchs—I met Gene Kelly's widow there—it is a place where I am always the youngest in the room. The wives, movie stars, and studio execs have been going to the same person every Monday for thirty years (indeed, in my interview with Jessica Vartoughian, the founder, she boasts of doing Tori Spelling's nails from age five). It is thanks to vanity that they have a relationship with fascinating women they otherwise would never know, women about whom they care deeply.

This is a unique setup but not entirely: Psychiatry also works because we only see those people once a week or month and never outside that room. That's why we feel free to tell them things we might not tell our family. As facialist Bebe Rudu confesses, they often feel the same about us.

Read, too, about Hollywood power manager Joy Gorman, single-handedly determined to keep Jane Tran's tiny Melrose nail shop alive. Then prepare to faint with pleasure at the strange and wonderful friendship between masseuse Asa Wrange and the ninety-three-year-old artist formerly known as Topsy Young.

Incredibly, for a book about beauty, our pages cover heartbreak, divorce, cutting, virginity, body dysmorphia, sexual abuse, and parental suicide. If the essays that emerged were not what I was expecting, the authors probably weren't expecting them either. Truth is an unpredictable trigger. You start thinking about your body and your body becomes a kind of detached witness. Memory monsters splash to the surface from water that looked clear.

Damage Control is real women talking about real things, with raw honesty and hope. I like to think it's the current climate. Yes, people want to kvetch. And polish. Distract. Go light and fluffy. They also want this type of permission—and articulation—of things maybe they hadn't faced, or realized. Here, in context of our human (so human) desire to be touched, make emotional connections, look pretty, healthy, desirable—the power of strangers.

—*Emma Forrest*

PART 1

Hair Grows

(*or* You Live and You Learn)

You Have to Understand My Hair

MINNIE DRIVER

You have to understand my hair. In order to fully contextualize this story, my hair requires your investment in it as a nonverbal but alarmingly expressive and independent character. Even as I sit here now it is fighting the fact that it is rooted to my scalp, and reaches out longingly as if each spiraling strand heard there was somewhere much better to be in the north, south, east, and west.

When I was at school, along with being called 50p face (a hexagonal British coin) I was also called Slash, Animal, and T-rex. These refer (in order) to: Guns N' Roses, the Muppets, and Marc Bolan. These were not always accurate reflections of my hair, however, and no one was more surprised than me when, with the hideous advent of boarding school, with no nanny or mum manning the hair dryer, my previously wavy, silky locks now doubled in size and corkscrewed madly around my face, giving my entire head the appearance of one gigantic exclamation point.

Remember for a moment the late seventies and early eighties—not the music or the clothes, not burgeoning Thatcherism, or indeed Ayatollahism—no, let's remember the hair gel; thick, radioactive-green gel in a clear tub, can't recall the name but it has to be the only one you too remember because there wasn't anything else. It is a credit to modern-day product development that I could make a realistic effigy of my entire family using only the hair product containers in my bathroom right now, and I thank God for it. That green gel back in the day had a simple protocol: First, it would solidify your hair to the density of concrete, then a fusing process would occur whereby one big dreadlock greeted you upon awakening. I was aware of the consequences of using the evil stuff, but with sweet naïveté and hope (which would only in my thirties be redefined as barking madness), I always believed there might be a different outcome to a repeated action.

And so I soldiered on through weddings and parties, a soft-focus fuzz in the back of pictures, always smiling, always wishing I had a hat. I looked at some of those pictures the other day and saw again the gaping chasm that physically exists between me and my mother and sister Kate; they were elongated blondes, graceful and contained, with huge smiles that were simultaneously warm and removed, they were Ariels to my Caliban, as sleek and unbothered as I was messy and impassioned. And both with the straightest hair you could imagine.

In the summer of 1984 my mother's marriage to my step-father was in its death throes, we had very little money, but in the close quarters of a tiny cottage in Hampshire, all any of us wanted to do was get away, anywhere, for some kind of holiday. A hotel was found in Arcachon, a seaside town in Bordeaux, and my mother, my sister, and I, along with our six-year-old brother, Ed (blond, curly-ish), set off to find respite from the emotional turmoil of rural England.

Our poor mother. Now, having experienced the kind of heartbreak that leaves your head resting gently against the bathroom floor, I understand the profound need to run away from pain; it must have been very difficult that we all decided to run away from pain with her. And so we arrived in the middle of the night at our third-floor hotel in Arcachon. A Chinese restaurant occupied the first two floors, and the air smelled dramatically of kung pao croissants. We woke up the next morning to a roar of traffic, ninety-degree heat, and the only French town I have ever known to be annoyingly perky. I remember we could all fit on the sliver of balcony if we stood in a horizontal line with our backs pressed up against the wall. Mum, determined to be bright, said everything was going to be fine and we were going to find a lovely beach. Her voice was pitched way too high to really believe the bit about it being fine, but the beach sounded all right. I stood dressing with my sister in front of the tiny mirror in the bathroom; she ran a hand through her long, blond hair, sighed, and adjusted the waistband of her shorts.

"Get dressed, Minnow."

"I am dressed."

"That's the T-shirt you slept in."

"I know, but it covers everything up."

"You're a loony."

I looked in the mirror, and her appraisal couldn't really be faulted. My T-shirt went to my knees and my hair was a crackling fizz, rebelling wildly at France and her maximum humidity.

On the beach, my T-shirt pulled over my knees, I sat looking at Kate. There, with tourists packed around her like a sunburnt sea, she looked dreamy, feline, and utterly perfect. At fourteen I genuinely believed if I could look like her, everything would be better; that without my freckled curves and fright-wig hair, the knot in my stomach would unfurl. The pitted road of popularity, boys, and the rest of my life would smooth into an open plain of charm and fortune. I knew so little of the inner workings of her mind and heart that her exterior was truly all I focused on, and so I guess it was with myself too.

We ate lunch in a horribly overpriced beach café, where my brother flung his sweaty cheese sandwich onto the floor. You couldn't blame him, even the cadaverous dog hanging out nearby for just such an occurrence wouldn't touch it.

"Well what *do* you want to eat then, Ed?"

"Strawberries."

"OK, we'll get strawberries."

They came, they looked bad, he ate them, and we headed back to our towels. Almost immediately Ed started to look green.

"I'm going to be sick, Mummy."

"No, no, no, don't be sick, darling, those were very expensive, delicious strawberries and you loved them."

"I'm going to be sick though."

And so it was. I realized we'd reached rock-bottom far sooner than we usually did on family trips, as I watched Mum holding Ed and simultaneously counting out the net worth of the strawberries.

"Ten francs! Oh darling, do stop . . . twenty! They cost almost 100 francs; you mustn't be sick anymore . . ." It was terribly funny and terrible at the same time. Ed threw up the last 80 francs, and as we sat down, I thought my mother was going to cry.

"Don't worry Mum, Min and I have money Dad gave us. We'll spend that."

"We'll do no such thing, that's your special money, come on, let's go and walk around town." Mum jumped to her feet, fully done with this particular nightmare and apparently eager for the next.

"I quite fancy cutting off all my hair," Kate said to no one in particular. "You know, like Siobhan from Bananarama."

"Well then let's find a hairdresser!" said Mum, suddenly reinvigorated by the thought of an actual plan. I was stupefied.

"Why would you cut off all your hair, you have perfect hair, I mean, it's perfect?"

"It's annoying," she said.

I was incensed. Annoying? Long, straight, blond hair annoying? It felt like sacrilege.

We wandered along the seafront, and there between two bars was a salon called La Jolie Fille. It looked fairly un-*jolie*, but there was a smiling man waving through the window so we went in. Inside was somewhere between a barber shop and a hairdresser's, and the waving man seemed to be the only person about.

"*Bonjour*," said Kate.

"*Je voudrais couper mes cheveux.*"

"*Ah bon, asseyez—vous mademoiselle.*"

Mum spoke perfect French and translated when Kate's schoolgirl version ran out. The man didn't know Siobhan from Bananarama but he had trimmed Nana Mouskouri's hair in the late seventies, so everyone felt we were pretty much good to go. I leaned against the sink and watched in fascinated horror as he tied her hair in a ponytail and then chopped it off. Her hair fell in a bobbed curtain around her cheekbones; he then took an electric razor and shaved the nape of her neck, then cut the hair on the back of her head to about an inch, and it all sloped fantastically, all the way down to the longer pieces around her face. She looked staggering and I felt tears burning at the backs of my eyes. It really wasn't how good she looked that made me sad. It was the complete confidence with which she'd just chopped it off and now the easy way in which she got up from the chair, brushed her lap, and said, "*Merci Monsieur.* Shall we go and get an ice cream, Mum?"

I gripped the sink. I wanted so much to be what I was not, and there in that empty hair salon I wondered if my butterfly wings just needed some help in being revealed.

"I think I'd quite like a haircut too." Mum and Kate looked at me.

"OK, darling, but do remember last time . . ." Mum trailed off.

"Your hair's quite hard to, you know . . ." Kate trailed off.

"I know but I'd like to. Now. Really, you go and get an ice cream and I'll stay here."

"Well, all right, but don't let him take too much off . . . *pas trop Monsieu, pas trop.*"

"*Bien Madame.*"

They left and I sat in the chair. We looked at each other in the mirror.

"*Je voudrais la Meme chose que ma soeur*, the same thing please."

He smiled and shrugged.

"*Mais, tu n'est pas ta soeur.*" (But, you are not your sister.)

I laughed. "*Evidament.*" (Obviously.)

"*S'il vous plait, Monsieur.*" (Please . . .)

He looked at me long and hard. He checked the spring in my (now) Afro.

"*La vie est une bonne ecole, peut-etre il en va de meme pour une coupe.*" (Life teaches us useful lessons, maybe it's the same with a haircut.)

Except I didn't understand what he said then.

He wet my hair down, and all I remember is that he cut it off. The razor buzzed, snip snip, snip . . . *et voilà.* My moon face looked back at me from the mirror; sleek dark hair grazing my hidden cheekbones. It looked so beautiful. I smiled.

"*Merci, merci Monsieur.*"

He patted my shoulder with a sweet kind of resignation and said, "*Tu dois attendre jusqu'a ce qui'l soit sec.*" (You must wait until it dries.)

I sat on the sea wall outside the salon waiting for Mum

and Kate and Ed. My neck felt naked and glorious. Finally,
finally I had done something about my own evolution, and my
new chic, sharp hairstyle was the proof. I swung my legs up
over the wall and crossed the road to wait under the salon's
awning, as it was meltingly hot. I caught sight of myself in the
window; my big white T-shirt, my Minnie Mouse beach bag,
and this strange helmet I hadn't previously been wearing. It
took me a second, and then with all the misery a fourteen-
year-old duckling can harbor, I started to cry. The man came
and got me off the sidewalk. He sat me in a chair, and my
reflection galvanized my hysteria. Where had the sleek dark
hair gone? Where was Clara Bow? How could the tight, frizzy
nonsense up around my ears now be my hair? How could bad
hair be worse? He patted my shoulder again.

"Tu est belle."

This made me cry even harder. The man seemed caught
between sadness and happiness.

*"D'accord, d'accord . . . tu sera belle, de votre proper ma-
niere, tu sera . . .* (All right, all right, you will be beautiful, in
your own way, you will be.) I took the scarf he handed me
and tied it like a fortune teller. My face with no hair around
it seemed open to me, blotchy and snotty and open. This, at
least, was something new. I carried on crying, but I heard him
say quietly, *"Ma petite, tu n'es pas tes cheveux."* (Sweetheart,
you are not your hair.) And truly, suddenly, without it . . . I
wasn't.

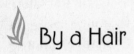 By a Hair

SAMANTHA DUNN

Hair cuttings are like splattered blood in that they are impossible to truly eradicate. Some evidence lingers, somehow. Escapes into crannies. Sticks under cabinets. Becomes camouflaged. It's exhausting, the business of trying to cleanse an environment of this biologic refuse, and so some remnant, however minuscule, will inevitably persist.

Hair and blood will always give you away. I can say this because I know something about both.

Blood I know because I am a woman, and we know of blood on bathroom tile. Not only am I a woman, but I once had my left leg nearly severed (truth) in a horseback-riding accident. Doctors put it back on; still, like I said . . . blood just everywhere. And I am also the niece of a shotgun suicide. My uncle, the man who, for much of my life, was the closest thing I had to a father, blew his head off with a 12-gauge in the lower paddock by the side of the barn. For years after that, if I really inspected the corrugated metal, I swear I could always find some tiny residuum of his crime against our family. Bone fragments, brains, arterial spurts—all of it, a damn nuisance.

But I digress. I'm stalling here, really. It's much easier for me to talk about traumatic death and menstruation and pain than it is for me to admit how I know about hair cuttings, and that's a strange fact.

I've noticed that in our confessional society of Dr. Phil and Oprah, on down to Jerry Springer and *Loveline* with Dr. Drew on the radio, we, as a people, have become habituated to relating the most explicit details of our emotional and sexual lives. Oral sex, childhood molestation, murderous anger for our spouses—we gleefully provide pictures and a soundtrack. But one item is never discussed: The money in our bank account. I've heard a woman tell of how she urinated on her husband to bring him to climax. But would this same woman admit, for example, that she had only $3.34 in her savings account, with $46.60 of overdrafts in checking until she gets paid on Monday? I've known one of my best friends for twenty-three years and yet I have no idea how much money she has ever made, whether she has an IRA, how much she pays in taxes. Revealing the amount of money we have or don't have is a great act of exposure, the final intimacy.

But why am I on this tangent? What's this got to do with hair?

I'm stalling again.

Maybe I should start at the beginning.

For the past decade I've lived on the tony West Side of

Los Angeles, with addresses that have included Malibu, the Pacific Palisades, the very hip Topanga Canyon. I'm a writer who has published four books, ghostwritten two others, had innumerable articles published in most of the glossy women's magazines, been a contributor to the celebrity bible, *InStyle*. I've been to the Oscars, the Grammys, the Emmys . . . etcetera, etcetera.

I mean for all of that to sound very glamorous and exciting, because I have been invested in presenting exactly that image to the world. I remember fantasizing about my glamorous life when I was a kid, sitting on my single bed in our home at Lot #78 in Enchanted Hills Mobile Home Park of Las Vegas, New Mexico, with the AstroTurf-covered front porch. We lived across the highway from a pasture and the town's one drive-in movie theater, respectively.

The fact that I was able to come from that and cobble together a glitzy-looking existence was not the result of any economic windfall. My West Side life was a product of great amounts of hard work, some luck, credit card debt, and even a bit of acting skill. And—this is very key—having *magnificent hair*.

In my world, you can get away with wearing torn jeans, funky jewelry, T-shirts—in Los Angeles all of that signals that you are a "creative," a nouvelle Bohemian, above or below the rules of the average pedestrian. Other details, like the in-shape body, can be fudged—you don't need to have a personal trainer to look like you have one, given enough discipline and motivation.

But a perfect cut, impeccable color, a mane that movie

stars would envy—that cannot be faked. This kind of hair is the signal to everyone that you *do* belong to an upper caste, you *have* achieved. It speaks of taste and genius and sex appeal, and says, "Never mind the cheap clothes, there's money and therefore power here—at the very least, a hidden trust fund."

Enter Terri, my stylist: a Georgia O'Keeffe who works in Clairol and L'Oréal, a Camille Claudel with scissors and a blow-dryer. The woman is a prodigy, truly, and Hollywood's elite—directors and actors and screenwriters who use Oscar statues for doorstops—line up at her private salon on Montana Avenue in Santa Monica to have her work brilliance on their heads. A cut and color from Terri costs more than a car payment, but most would gladly pay more if she asked them.

Terri and I became friends some years ago. We'd often pass each other with a bright hello at the stables where we both boarded our horses. My horse, a broken-down ex-racehorse that, like myself, I had spit-polished to look like a successful Thoroughbred; hers, a Western Pleasure show horse with a pedigree and flashy coat. One day she paused to chat about some horse-related item, the kind of thing only women who never outgrew their childhood pony fixation would be interested in. I remember she had unexpectedly reached to touch the auburn mop on my head—that day I had worn it down, uncharacteristically, not pulled back and stuck under my baseball cap.

"Girl, you've got hair some women would kill for," she said as her fingers worked through the frayed strands to pull them back over my ears. I recall it was a strange feeling—her gesture so familiar, so private, something like the touch of a lover but done with such cool, professional detachment, as if she were a jeweler appraising an uncut stone.

Terri let her hands drop. "But you've got to come see me. Any old time, I'll fit you in."

So I took her up on it, and after the first time I was hooked. Never mind that going to her wiped out my grocery budget for a month—I would go hungry to walk out of her salon feeling as sexy as Rita Hayworth, as pulled together as Princess Di. But going to Terri wasn't just about looking good on the outside—from the minute I sat in her chair I felt in the presence of a wise soul, the loving older sister I wish I had had to guide me through life. We talked of men and marriages, of childhood and mothers, of divorce and sex and careers and tears. Seeing Terri once a month was like going to a great psychoanalyst who also had a magic wand to turn me into beautiful—at least until my next shampoo.

Thanks to Terri, my glamour quotient went up. My income, however, did not. I was hanging on to my West Side life by a hair, as it were—my freelancer's paychecks irregular and perpetually late, the cost of living ever rising.

Then, it just snapped.

It wasn't one catastrophe but a series of seemingly random events, hubris, and bad decisions that hurled me into a true financial collapse. One big assignment didn't come through when an editor changed her mind about the topic, I was hired to write a book proposal but the client didn't pay . . . and then there was the decision to spend three months writing a play because there was a chance it would be picked up by some bigwigs with deep pockets. I was playing the odds. I lost.

There was more in the midst of this—the death of my beloved horse, disastrous romances, illness, catastrophes within
my family . . . let me just say there were many shovels burying
me under. In one year I managed to earn just $22,000 before
taxes. Bankrupt? Of course. I lost all forms of insurance. I
would have lost my car if it hadn't been paid off. I found a
room to rent; I explained that I was "downsizing." Truth: I
was living on a wage that would have supported me if I had
stayed in the trailer in New Mexico, but did not begin to sus-
tain even the barest essentials of life on the Pacific Coast.

Terri was witness to the plagues that entered my life, or
rather the plagues that I created, and knew how corrosive
each was to me. Stress and lack of nutrition made my hair fall
out in her hands. I could never really afford her but now not
at all, so I tried to cancel my appointments. She seemed put
out—we were friends. Had I found a new stylist? Did I not
like something she'd done? Of course not, I assured her, but I
couldn't think of good excuses. Finally I admitted to Terri and
only to Terri just how destitute I was.

"Oh just come on in, girl," she said to me. She didn't seem
shocked or rattled; she didn't judge or lecture. "I'll just shape
you up some. You're down but you don't have to look like it."

I don't know which one of us brought it up first, but I do
know that Terri was the one who worked out the plan. Here
was the deal: I was broke. She wanted to save money because
the lease was going up on her salon. This was the ideal for-
mula to set up a barter economy: Why didn't I become the
cleaning woman for her salon in exchange for her services?

I could maintain appearances, look like I had it all together even though I was a walking mess.

Her salon is a private nest above a French provincial restaurant and across the hall from a chi-chi yoga studio. In my sweatpants and T-shirt, my hair pulled back tightly from my face, I went in at night after all the nearby businesses had closed. I told myself it would be easier that way because I'd have the place to myself—there would be no interruptions—but it was because I could not reconcile what I was doing with who I thought I was.

Life and what you've made of it is harder to face in the daylight. For a long time I had been operating under the belief that my career and my fancy addresses meant I had transcended a past that still, well into my thirties, was a wellspring of pain and shame. But with my hands in soapy water and my back bent scrubbing Terri's floor, that belief was impossible to hold on to.

At night I scrubbed, and I scrubbed. I learned that cut hair is a potentially hazardous substance; it can work into your skin like fiberglass fragments and filter into your system. People who work in salons must wear close-toed shoes because exposure to hair cuttings can be toxic over time. In the daylight, however, I walked into the salon and took a seat in Terri's chair just like any other client.

Over the weeks, however, something began to shift within me. At the end of the night, although my back hurt and my shoulders felt tired, I felt a rush of accomplishment in creating order and cleanliness out of the chaos I found there each time. It also gave me a degree of joy to think of how happy

Terri would be when she walked into her space and found it beautiful—and I, accurate or not, imagined the feelings she herself had each day. That's what Terri does—she makes people more beautiful and raises their sense of well-being by whatever degree possible.

The three hours it took me to clean became a kind of meditation—all manner of thoughts and feelings unfolded in front of me for examination. One that continued to resurface: Why did I feel like some kind of Jay Gatsby—meaning, why had I tried for so long to fulfill certain expectations, find the right camouflage, so I could fit into what I was not? Why did I think slipping into this world of celebrity and sushi and BMWs was the solution to anything, anyway?

Change, for me, happens the way icebergs melt. Imperceptible thawing happens over time, then—*splash!*—something falls away.

So there I was, sitting in Terri's salon and waiting for her to finish with a client—I think she was going to give me lowlights that day. She had just finished with the razors on this client, who was, in the oblique way of the über-successful Hollywood denizen, talking about his nomination for an Oscar—he was a director; he'd already won the Golden Globe for his film.

"Sam's a really successful author . . ." Terri, ever the networker, began to tell this director. As she spoke she shook the hair from the protective apron around the man's neck. Without thinking, I went to the back and got the broom.

When I returned, they were both looking at me—Terri amused, the director unsure.

I shrugged. "I'm going to have to pick this stuff up later, so

I might as well do it now," I said, and began sweeping. In the mirror in front of us, my eyes caught the director's. In that moment I didn't give a good goddamn if he was enjoying the irony of the successful-author-as-cleaning-woman. It hit me that what I really wanted, wanted more than anything, was not to seem like a successful author, but to be a successful person.

There's not a lot more to tell. Eventually work started to improve and Terri got a new cleaning woman. One of my books is being made into a television movie, and I started teaching. And I'm thinking about writing another book. I also fell in love, deep and real and true, to a guy who likes to go to Angels baseball games and keeps corndogs in the freezer. We got married and moved to Orange, California, where there is no view of the beach and we don't know any celebrities, but we do go horseback riding together, and we take his kids to IHOP for pancakes on the weekends.

Terri sent me an e-mail yesterday to say hi and to check in. I forgot to mention that I bought her flashy Western show horse—she didn't have the time or inclination to ride anymore. In the e-mail she reminded me that I need to come to her and get my color done, because my auburn color wanes to a peculiar shade of yellow if allowed to fade for long enough. I told her I'd come in when I could manage it.

I do feel richer today, although I can't say that I have all that much more money (as of right now, $122.33 in the checking account). I can't say if I am anywhere close to becoming that successful person I yearned to be in that instant of meeting the director's eye. Maybe—as that old commercial used to say—only my hairdresser will ever know for sure.

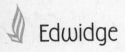 Edwidge

HELEN OYEYEMI

My hairdresser Edwidge is from the Ivory Coast. She is young, she speaks French and English interchangeably, she is beautiful and slim, starting, from my mirror perspective, from her fingers and continuing on to every part of her. She is pregnant at the moment, and her baby will be stunning. Also, Edwidge has Skills. In a departure from other hair salons that offer Beyonce weaves and Gabrielle Union-esque styling for relaxed hair, the East London hair salon I go to caters only to black women who make the slightly harder choice to drop out of the accepted beauty hierarchy altogether and wear their hair unstraightened, or "natural." My hair history has been checkered to the extent that by the time I came for a consultation with her I wasn't sure whether my hair was natural or not. All I knew was that if Edwidge had said there was nothing she could do for me, I would have been at a complete loss as to what else to do to try to find a tolerable self-image. I had been chemically straightening my hair on and off since I was twelve, and from there I'd hidden it away in braided hair extensions so I didn't have to think about it. My hair was getting me down down down. My hair should have been a mess, falling out in handfuls, or if not that, steaming with neglect and radiation—anything but natural. But there's something about my family's hair that pushes chemicals right out (there are rumors of "a wavy-haired *Arab*" far back in my mum's side of the family. In two years, without knowing it, I'd grown out the lye from root to tip. Edwidge cooed over my hair and set about putting it to rights, washing, combing, and oiling so that within the hour I was looking at myself as I'd never dared to properly do before. And, oh God, genuine African princess, beyond stereotype, yes! But no one else in the salon even looked twice at me—everyone in that place had amazing hair—frizzy and loose, or glossy, bulky plaits, or soft china bumps. I wanted dreadlocks. This decision may or may not have been influenced by the awe-inspiring crowns worn by Suzan-Lori Parks, Lauryn Hill, and Toni Morrison, my alternative black diasporic heroes. I came back to Edwidge the following weekend so that she could backcomb my hair—O black hair salon, bastion of middle-class blackness, where you pay good money for someone to quickly, stylishly, and irredeemably tangle your hair so you can go home and have your mum squint and say, "Are you becoming a Rasta? I hope you didn't pay for that."

Edwidge has got hair stories, stories of pain and horror—

her own hair, which she plaits herself, is bulky and curled so tightly that she needs help combing it and often cries and gets headaches after the combing process. I asked her if she'd tried straightening it, and she gave me a sage nod. "Yeah, but on hair like mine it doesn't work, you know, it doesn't last." I am in awe of Edwidge. If hair runs parallel to personality (and some part of me thinks it does), I'd call her a powerhouse. Her hair kicks foreign influences out of its system, plus she is the fairy godmother of my hair, plus she doesn't seem to accept any of the significance imposed upon her beauty by others. (One time when she was in the middle of retwisting my now adolescent dreadlocks, a guy came into the salon and made kissy faces at her and said, "You're gorgeous," and she couldn't stop laughing. But the guy could see, and I could see in the mirror, that she was trying to say something. When she recovered from her laughing fit, she managed to say it: "And so?")

I was watching *Britain's Next Top Model* the other day. That's right! *Britain's Next Top Model*—God made that show. Those girls are Nietzschean scapegoats; they suffer so we don't have to. The girls have reached the stage where hair-dressers and makeup artists take them in hand and demolish the things that make their faces real—split ends, short eye-lashes, tufty brow lines—in order to drag the diamond out of the rough. All that's left of these girls by the end of the day is unmussed hair that moves in one slick direction, pair after pair of fierce eyes, shiny pouts, all focused around the common feature that got them picked for the contest in the first place: insane cheekbones. Cheekbones with the kind of definition that sells anything, any brand—*buy this perfume or I will most certainly find you and cut you with my face, bitch.* But often hair must die so that these kinds of cheek-bones might live to their full effect. The death of hair is very very serious. Many men are demoralized by balding; many women are paralyzed by scissors. So the *Next Top Model* girls sat around and giggled as they watched their faces turn into masks, but when faced with the chop, one girl looked at her new, short hairstyle in the mirror, went outside, and burst into tears. The other wannabe models said little in reaction to this, but the words "silly cow" were palpable in the air. My feeling was that the crying girl wasn't being idiosyncratic in her response to a hair change that she hadn't called the shots over; she was being more honest than the other girls. Those other girls are the silly cows. How do you know how you're doing inside, whether you're a girl at any given point or not, what kind of girl you are if you as a girl don't have control over your hair?

Some examples:

- When I was between the ages of eight and eleven, my dad regularly cropped my hair as short as a boy's. I sulked and pleaded, but every month he sat me down in a nest of newspaper and went at my hair with scissors. Some months, if I behaved too badly about it, he shaved my head. My dad believed that this was the number one method for scaring prospective boyfriends away from me. I suffered. I suffered tearlessly and in the all-consuming, disbelieving way that only a preadolescent can, until after a conversation with my mother over the embarrassment of having people come up to me and ask me whether I was boy or girl, my father allowed me to wear small gold hoop earrings. I think I only realized the extent to which I felt stripped of something vital with each haircut when, during my suicide attempt at fifteen, the first thing I did before taking several handfuls of ibuprofen was cut all my (then relaxed) shoulder-length hair off with scissors. Overriding self-image: irrelevant, as control was out of my hands.

- At first I was happy with having my hair relaxed (by this I mean chemically straightened) because it was easy to comb and I could wear it in a lot of the hairstyles that the pretty white girls wore. Then the relaxed hair became ugly to me. It's difficult to explain what the problem was, other than that my hair just didn't frame my face the way it should have. My hair always seemed separate from me. I always felt as if it was coming loose from my scalp, but when I checked with a comb, it never was. I dreaded mirrors and photographs. I read *The Autobiography of Malcolm X* and my hair became a mutant helmet, deceptively soft but meaning me harm. I knew I had to be rid of it but I couldn't bear the thought of cropping it short again, as if the action would call up some Pavlovian response in me and I'd mindlessly scramble headfirst into the medicine cupboard, looking for pills. Overriding self-image: subhuman.

- My braided hair extensions felt better; when my fingers strayed to the base of each plait I could feel curls balled up like tiny fists. I wore very long, white-streaked braids, blue braids, plum purple braids, red; and I felt unique. I was probably encouraged to this feeling by the Japanese tourists who would stop me on the streets of Cambridge and ask if they could take photographs of my hair. Overriding self-image: interesting, but is it pretty?

The quest for pretty. The hassle my mum went through with my sister and me when we were younger. Every other minute we were asking to have our hair relaxed. She asked us why. She said, "It'll ruin your hair." She'd had her hair relaxed when she was younger and now she's constrained to maintaining it, retouching the perm every couple of months. By the time she buckled under our urgency and my dad was resigned to it, our mum decided to do our hair at home. Rather than send us to salons and spend up to 80 pounds each on small and ignorant heads, my mum plastered our hair with lye products and fried our hair straight herself. Relaxed hair was great! It was silky and soft and moved in the wind, unlike our natural curls, which grew upward and stood unperturbed by sun, rain, or out-and-out storm. Mary and I wanted long, straight hair, as limp as possible, and in the days before my mum agreed to relax our hair, we'd run around the house with towels arranged on our heads so that they fell to our shoulders like hair. Sometimes we'd bunch the towels into ponytails or pigtails. My sister (now eighteen) will wish disfigurement upon me if she finds out I'm writing about this. What's embarrassing is how painfully we felt our natural hair to be ugly. What's redeeming is how positive we were in building constructive bridges to change that. We didn't let ourselves feel unhappy that we were black kids with tough bushy hair—though Mary did win the Boots Most Beautiful Baby Competition for 1989 and her curls were actually achingly beautiful, regardless of whether we apprehended this at the time. No, we skipped the sadness after the realization that we weren't cute and used the towels and our pleas to have our hair straightened as projects for change. We were plucky kids. Enid Blyton might have written stories about girls like me and Mary if she had been (a) remotely interested in the inner lives of girls and

(b) not writing stories in which hideous black golliwogs were rewarded for good behavior by being made "clean" (and white) by "magic rain."

At school my hair's failure to grow downward made me not at all an outcast but a social boy. How can you be bitter when your best friends are the unwitting recipients of societal advantages without being involved in their causation? So I say the following without bitterness: The white girls in my primary school class set the standard for cuteness. Boys who fancied these girls would tug their plaits or ponytails in the playground—the white girls often fussed over each other's hair. When I was nine, the cleverest boy in the class approached me to tell me that he fancied me. All the other girls and that boy's friends said it was true, and they wanted to know, what was I gonna do? So apparently the boy did really like me. But I didn't know about that, I wasn't convinced, and I wasn't going to make a fool of myself by liking him too rashly back. My skepticism came from a lack of prior signaling—he didn't yank my hair or pinch me—but now I think I might have been a little bit physically unapproachable. To affectionately yank my hair, you would actually have had to bury a fist in it, and that's commitment, that's not a casual pull. Edwidge makes that commitment. Unlike the salons where I've sat for up to eight hours with my head under the hands of a taciturn woman who adds extensions to my hair without comment or conversation, Edwidge takes on my hair in handfuls, both literally and in a more general sense. *We talk hair.* We talk lots of other things too, and complain about the hair salon Muzak, but we talk hair. Ours and other people's. It's not the playground fussing with silky straight hair that I used to long to join in on, but it performs the same function in the relationship between me and my hair. Edwidge's attentions bring my hair to my notice—it's pretty, it's real, it's there, and it belongs to me.

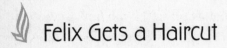 Felix Gets a Haircut

MAGGIE PALEY

To quote Lola Montez, the celebrated Irish-Spanish dancer and adventuress (1818–1861) whose beauty advice is collected in *The Arts of Beauty or Secrets of a Lady's Toilet*: "I have known women, who had scarcely another charm to commend them, to carry off scores of hearts by a bountiful and beautiful head of hair."

There are some women who have worn their hair the same way for their entire lives. For the rest of us a haircut is a chance to experience transformation. I, for one, am almost always thoroughly sick of myself by the time I schedule a haircut. I count on my haircutter to perform a metamorphosis; and because people are fallible, I know that even the greatest haircutter is capable of giving a bad haircut. No matter how wonderful I may look in the haircutter's mirror, wearing a gold-colored robe, bathed in soft, artfully placed light, I perch on the haircut seat filled with trepidation. Sometimes, as I watch my hair being snipped, I'm horrified to hear myself piping up to supervise. "Don't make it too short." "Aren't you going to cut the bangs?" "Can it be a little shorter in back?" How would I like it if someone tried to tell me how to write a story as I was writing it? Come to think of it, someone does— my inner editor, the voice of the censor. I know I need to quiet her if I hope to do any decent work—and yet when she wants to interrupt a haircut to put in her two cents, I allow her to speak aloud.

I was reminded of my own behavior the other day, when my cat Felix had his hair cut by Howard Bedor, New York's premiere professional cat groomer.

Howard brought his suitcase on wheels upstairs. He arranged his scissors and combs on the shelf above the tub in the kitchen, preparing to grapple with Felix on the white Formica tub top. Felix doesn't like people messing with his hair—his coat was matted because he'd refused to let me comb him properly. He's also suspicious of strangers in the house, and he'd hid in the back of my closet the minute the doorbell rang. I sympathized. Every haircut is a turning in the road; it might go right but it might go wrong, and then what will you do? Yet we human adults consider ourselves too dignified to hide in our closets when the time comes.

Howard has been cutting cats' hair at home, without sedative since 1986, and he came prepared. Over his white T-shirt with its Howard Bedor logo (an HB on its side, with the loops of the Bs made into cats' eyes), he put on a plastic apron decorated with drawings of cats. He put wristbands on his wrists.

He sheathed his forearms in cotton and Kevlar sleeves, of the sort used in the construction industry, and over these he pulled on a pair of suede welders' sleeves. Next came a pair of fingerless gloves, the kind Michael Jackson used to wear. Over the first pair of gloves he put a second; these were more like mitts, or boxing gloves with fingers, and they were bright yellow. Welders' gloves, he said, covered with duct tape. Now he was ready for Felix. Outlandish as his getup was, at least, I thought, he knew what he was in for, unlike those who cut the hair of humans and are subject to verbal attacks.

I led Howard to the closet, and he grabbed Felix with his mitts. Felix struggled, but Howard knows how to hold a cat. He carried Felix to the tub top, put him down, and held him there, one of his yellow mitts bearing down on Felix's neck, pinning him in place like a nut around a bolt. Felix struggled and yowled, Howard held fast. "This is like arm wrestling," Howard said. "The cat is going to lose."

Once Felix quieted down Howard dressed him in an Elizabethan collar, one of those clear plastic funnels you sometimes see around the head of a dachshund, that keeps him from biting himself after surgery. This one would keep Felix from biting Howard.

Howard began to comb and snip; Felix began to hiss and wail, to scream bloody murder, really, as if someone were after him with an axe. Once I was on an airplane going from Houston to Mexico City, and there was a man in his early twenties sitting a few rows in front of me who began to scream the moment the plane began to taxi down the runway. It became clear from the rhythmic, almost ritual nature of his screaming that this young man was disturbed, and the man next to him, who apparently was his keeper, kept trying to shush him. But the odd thing was that the screams, while hard on the eardrums, were calming to the psyche; the screamer was voicing the fears that we all felt and so the rest of us could relax. In the same way I felt that Felix, splayed on the tub top with a plastic Elizabethan funnel collar around his neck, was screaming for all of us who'd ever had our hair cut by someone we didn't trust, but we couldn't protest properly, because the don't-touch-me scream had long ago been civilized out of us.

Howard's technique was two-pronged. On the one hand, he knew how to cut cat hair. On the other, he knew how to show a cat who was boss. KMA, Kitty Martial Arts, he called it; he would let the cat have the illusion he was in charge—as a human haircutter is bound to do with a client—until the crunch arrived. Felix kept up his wailing—Howard assured me he wasn't being hurt, it was just his ego talking—and finally, about mid-haircut, he seemed to have broken free. He leaped from the table—but Howard's hand was still on him, and he was stopped midair, suspended at the end of Howard's arm. He was still screaming when Howard put him back on the table. "I like him," Howard said. "He has a lot of spirit."

Nevertheless, by the time Howard was finished, he was sweating so much he had to change his T-shirt. Felix was shorn on his left flank and his belly, where the mats had been; the rest of his coat was still long. If only he'd been cooperative, I thought, Howard could have worked swiftly and shaped his hair. As it was, his cut was far from stylish.

I asked Howard if cats were vain. I asked this because

Felix is always posing, lying stretched on the white floor like a pinup on a leopard skin, turning his yellow eyes on me in what can only be a flirtatious gesture. But Howard said no. Cats weren't vain about what they looked like, only about the way they felt inside. Of course that's what humans are supposed to become, once we're fully evolved. But no matter how evolved you are, it's hard to live with a lopsided haircut.

Putting yourself in the hands of a haircutter is an act of trust. And the best haircuts, I would venture to say, are collaborations. It's important to let the haircutter know you trust him or her; say what you need to about what you'd like—be articulate and explicit and then shut up and surrender. Difficult as it sometimes seems, in order to get a good haircut you need to let the haircutter do it.

As for Felix—maybe he isn't vain about his looks, and he's certainly a happier cat now that Howard has snipped off his matted hair. But when friends come over these days he sits uncharacteristically still, showing them his good side.

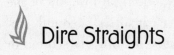 Dire Straights

JUDY FORREST

"I think she should have it done," said Dr. Sweeting. Dr. Sweeting was the principal of Joan of Arc Junior High School, where my mother taught phys ed and dance. She took Dr. Sweeting's advice on absolutely everything.

Dr. Sweeting was tall and grand, with commanding, no-nonsense features. She seemed to sweep rather than walk, to make entrances and exits rather than come and go. Recently she had thought I should have a kitten and had brought one to our house, sweeping in to make the delivery and sweeping out to her next appointment. We loved the cat but didn't know anything about how to look after her. I named her Beauty. After a year, she went mad. She rarely came out from under the bed, and when she did, she hissed and scratched so you couldn't get near her. Finally, not knowing what else to do, we gave her to the SPCA. Years later, after my parents had died, my aunts told me that Beauty wasn't a girl at all; she was a "tom." My parents hadn't wanted me to know this. I've never figured out why.

I'm not sure what Dr. Sweeting was doing at Joseph's Beauty Parlor on that autumn day in the early fifties. Certainly not having her hair done. Had she traveled from the school on Ninety-third Street down to Eighty-fifth and Columbus just to advise on whether I should have my hair straightened? Possibly. I do remember that she thought it was a good idea, waving me onto a train that wouldn't come to a full stop until the day that JFK was assassinated.

I sat in the chair, waiting for Joseph to begin. I knew that the process would not make my hair a soft caramel red like my mother's, but I hoped that it might make the texture more like hers: wavy rather than kinky. You don't hear the word *kinky* applied to hair these days, but that's what it was: kinky, with fuzzy, flyaway bits at the top. Once I was introduced to one of the teachers at my mother's school; she gasped and said, "But your hair!"

Joseph was a Polish refugee. He was kind and serious, almost solemn. His hair was a luxurious strawberry blond, but that's the only thing about him that seemed right for a hairdresser. The rest was more like some kind of repairman. He began applying the straightening cream, telling me to let him know if it stung. It did sting. I pointed to the places on my scalp where it burned and Joseph applied soothing oil on a Q-tip. The fumes made me cough. My mother watched and chewed her lip.

The result was certainly straight. Totally, relentlessly

straight. Not a curve anywhere. It hung, dragging the rest of my face with it. My mother looked doubtful as she rose to pay and take me home. "No, not yet," Joseph said. "I wouldn't leave her like that." He clipped some rubber rollers into my hair and placed me under the dryer. The result was somewhat better. It had a little more body, but it still lay flat against my head. And I have learned something about myself. Because my hair was so wide, I'd always assumed it was thick. It isn't. It's thin. Kinky but thin. This was before the beauty industry had learned to refer to thin hair as fine.

In the morning it was almost entirely straight again. There was no point pretending that I was sick and couldn't go to school. I'd have to go eventually, and anyway, maybe my friends would like it. Mostly they were just stunned. "Wow!" "How did that happen?" "It sure is straight!" Carole, my best friend, had more of an opinion: "Your hair looks awful. It looks like a wet dishrag." After school, one of the more outspoken mothers said, "I think they went a little too far."

In the next few months, Joseph got a somewhat better fix on it. He used Dep, which was called a setting lotion back then and is still around today as a styling gel. The biggest problem was the condition of my straightened hair, which you couldn't get a comb through without a truckload of conditioner that made it limp.

After two months, the new growth prompted a decision: Should I have it done again? The choice was fuzzy with body or straight but limp. There was nothing in between. Without consulting Dr. Sweeting, I went for straight but limp. None of my friends, and none of the movie stars in *Modern Screen*

Magazine, had kinky hair. So the routine was built: straight-
ener, neutralizer, rollers, dryer. Between straightening sessions, Joseph would do just a set and sometimes a trim. And
between those sets with Joseph, I did it myself. I tried everything, every style, every parting, every kind of roller, every
lotion. I tried to create dips and bangs, ponytails, pageboys,
flips. Sometimes I thought, *Yes, this is the answer*, but it never really was. My mother's hair had straightened with puberty
but mine did not.

After a couple of years, Joseph moved on and I moved up
the street to a different beauty parlor (we didn't yet call them
salons) recommended by Helen, one of the teachers at Joan
of Arc. I guess Dr. Sweeting had other things to attend to. My
mother liked the cut of Helen's hair, failing to factor in that
Helen's hair was short, thick, wavy, and nothing like mine.

At the new place I had Pamela and then Mary Lou. Pamela
was in her thirties, blond and Monroe-ish. Another beautician (we didn't yet have stylists) told me that Pamela claimed
to be an Indian princess. She was something of a diva. One
time I put my hand to my hair as she was working and she
shouted, "It's a terrible thing to touch it before I've finished.
Terrible."

Mary Lou was more like Gloria Grahame: slim, thin-
lipped, and direct. Sometimes, between straightenings, my
hair would revert to its fuzzy self, especially at the top. "Can't
you make it lie flat?" I asked Mary Lou. "Yeah," she said. "Get
me a hammer and some nails."

And then I was seventeen and off to college near Boston,
where the beauticians were less ready to engage. I went to

some salon with my hair pinned up in what I thought was a French twist, like Grace Kelly. The receptionist sent me to a hairdresser who blanched when my hair was unleashed. "I had no idea," the receptionist apologized. "She had it scrunched up. I didn't know." After that I only had my hair done when I went back to New York on holidays. There were lots of nice girls in my dorm and we shared our equipment. I used big rollers, held in place with clips or bobby pins, on wet hair. Then I dried it with a hand dryer, which took a long time and was hard on my right arm, but the result wasn't too bad. If I could have stayed inside all the time, I'd have been fine. But I was a slave to the weather. If the day was humid, it was back to the frizz that I'd worked so hard to discourage. If you don't have frizzy hair you have no idea how mortifying it is to step outside with one hairstyle and be kidnapped by another. You have no control. Your destiny wins every time.

After college, I returned to New York and got a job. We still lived near Columbus Avenue, but I moved my hair to a salon on the more desirable East Side, run by Richard and Rose. Rose was like Ethel Merman. Richard was also like Ethel Merman. I don't know why, but they were always terribly overbooked. You could wait for anything up to an hour, while Richard complained, "I don't know what Rose had on her mind, overbooking me like this." I don't think they were very good or even very popular; they were just disorganized and understaffed. Also, they were well placed for the discount designer stores.

I can't remember much about the salon that came after Richard and Rose. I'm not sure where it was, and its personnel remain blurred. Sometimes the place comes into focus—then it's gone, like Brigadoon. What I do know is that I was there on the afternoon of November 22, 1963, having my hair straightened in preparation for my wedding the following week. I also remember the protective gown, a pale green nylon. They had a radio going in the background, and the news broke just as the lotion went on—first that he was shot and then that he was dead. I stood up, ripped off the gown, and ran for my coat. "You can't go," the hairdresser shouted after me. "We haven't put the neutralizer on." But I was off. I don't know why but I imagined there would be violence and looting, and I needed to be home. We thought of calling off the wedding out of respect, but we didn't. My hair broke off my head in great chunks.

As long as the wedding was going ahead, I would have to do something about my hair. That's when I moved farther upmarket to Kenneth at Henri Bendel, near the St. Regis, where I was getting married. My stylist was Carl, the first out-there gorgeous gay boy I'd ever known. He had golden hair and mascara, and when I arrived, he was modeling a fur coat given to him by a lover for being "very very good." He grew quiet when he saw the wreckage of my hair—a microcosm of the grieving nation. Carl was sweet and funny and talented. He introduced me to the technique that was to become a significant part of my life for the next twenty-five years: blow-drying. I almost forgot about JFK as I watched lock after lock relax and flow from a broken nest into a swathe of satin. I never had my hair chemically straightened again. I was still a slave to the weather but I'd never cared for the outdoors any-

way. There were taxis, hats, umbrellas, and a variety of smart
head scarves for emergencies. Carl told me that Jackie Ken-
nedy, whose hair was done by Kenneth himself, also had thin
hair that tended to frizz; hence all the scarves and falls.

My relationship with Carl lasted longer than my marriage.
But not forever. I don't know why I moved on. Carl persuad-
ed me to have my neck waxed (the first and last time I ever
had anything waxed), but it wasn't because of that. I think it
must have been a sort of sixties Zeitgeist, or maybe a being-
in-my-twenties Zeitgeist, or possibly a recently divorced Zeitgeist: You're not unhappy but you want to try something new.
So I switched to Vidal Sassoon and Clay. Clay was lovely—
cheerful and unpretentious. He was six-foot-four, which is really too tall for a hairstylist; you can never lift the client's chair
high enough, especially if, like me, the client is short. Clay
approached this difficulty by adopting a unique stance. He
would stand on the inside of his ankles with his knees bent inward. I don't know how he did it, but he managed. The chair
next to Clay was manned by Alex, who was not only camp
but British. He taught us Cockney rhyming slang. "Clock the
boat on that one coming up the apples," he'd say, and I was
enchanted. I tried it around town but I sounded like Eliza
Doolittle in reverse.

Sometimes Alex would help by tackling one side of my hair
while Clay did the other. Between them, they could just about
achieve that Mary Quant–Peggy Moffat–Rudi Gernreich look
that I so craved. When I washed my own hair, it took an entire
evening and many hours with the hand dryer. It was OK from
the front, but whenever I gathered the courage to view my

hair from the side or the back, I was twelve again. So I had it done more often.

Then three things happened at about the same time. A friend told me about a new trend: the natural look. If your hair was frizzy, you let it be frizzy. The Afro was crossing cultures from Angela Davis to Dory Previn. I found this hard to accept. For years there had been only one look; was I really being excused? Pardoned? Set free? I resisted.

Then Clay changed his name to Cliff. He'd been to see a numerologist who had told him that he needed to be Cliff, not Clay. Then Alex decided he was straight. This was not gradual. One week he was camping around in a fluffy sweater and the next he was all preppie, speaking with a completely different voice, and getting married to a very nice and gifted young actress. Soon he was a father. They are probably still together.

With change in the air, Cliff and I decided that we would cut my hair and wear it natural. Going back to the office after lunch that day was like the day I'd gone into school with my hair newly straightened. It really was quite extreme: a perfectly round Afro, short, high, and wide. My best friend, Laurie, said, "I told you from the start I liked your hair the way it was." The men seemed to like it better. "Wear it like you believe it," Cliff had said. But that was the problem. I didn't believe it. The real me wasn't the me I wanted. So we returned to blow-drying and I remained a slave. We didn't yet have the phrase *fashion victim*.

I stayed with Cliff until 1972 when, on a whim that gained momentum, I moved to London for a year. I found a job, a flat in Marylebone, and a salon nearby. It was called Jingles and my stylist was Jason. I was a Jingles Belle, and I learned that instead of bangs, I had a fringe. Jason looked like Brian May. He was a mass of curls but he was happy to blow-dry my hair as straight as it would go.

Instead of going back to New York after a year, I bought a flat in South Kensington and married again. The ceremony and reception were small and understated but I still had to have my hair done. I'd moved to a salon near the flat, where my hair was done by Nick. I looked at my wedding pictures recently and my hair looks OK, except for an oddly rolled fringe. When my daughter was born, I took her in to see Nick, who marveled at her spectacular head of curls. Today one of my daughters wears her hair curly while the other uses a variety of tongs and hats to make it straight.

Twenty-five years ago today, I met Peter. I would know this even if he hadn't just called to wish me a happy anniversary. I was seven months' pregnant with my second daughter and having my hair done at a salon called Harambee, a tall, thin house just off South Moulton Street. My stylist was Oliver, but when I arrived that day, Oliver had called in sick. Peter presented himself and said, "Why not give us a try?" So I did. Peter was a bit like Clay, tall and easygoing.

For the first few years, Peter dutifully straightened my hair with the blow-dryer, but not quite so straight, so it didn't have so far to go when the weather hit. Then we cut it quite a bit shorter, and for the first time, I was able to manage it myself by using a cordless styler instead of a dryer.

Over the past quarter century, Peter and I have talked about child development, GCSEs, A-levels, university, politics, and movies. I've followed him to three different salons and have seen him age not at all. He has seen my hair go gray and even more fine. The gray is easy enough to cover but the thinning hair responds less and less well to straightening techniques. A few years ago, the anti-frizz market really took off with lotions, gels, and sprays that made it possible for formerly fuzzy hair to dry, undisturbed, into curls. So Peter and I decided to have another go at the natural look. Rain and high humidity no longer ruin my life and I have made my peace with destiny. If I were young, I would wear it long like Minnie Driver, but when I do, I look like Bette Davis in *Whatever Happened to Baby Jane?*, so we keep it short.

Something else happened today, in addition to Peter's anniversary call. Over fifty years since Joseph first applied that sulphurous mixture to my misfit's mop, my younger daughter tells me about a salon in Covent Garden where fashionistas pay 250 pounds ($435) to have their hair chemically straightened. I am troubled. If people are willing to pay that kind of money, straight hair must matter, after all. Have I been in denial? Is "natural" just a euphemism for unfortunate? I hear an authoritative swish on the other side of the door. It's Dr. Sweeting, sweeping in from Beyond. "I think," she says "that you should have it done."

PETER THEOBALD
Hairdresser

Peter works in London, going home on the weekend to Lewes, where he lives with his sister, a single mother who moved in with Peter, his mother, and his father when her son, Nicholas, was two. He's now twenty-three, and Peter remains the father figure in his life.

I do cut the family's hair. Nicholas has never had a haircut other than mine. But they always have to remind me because I don't notice when they need haircuts—that's part of my cutting off when I leave the salon.

I don't make a great fortune but I have a good lifestyle—I can take five weeks off. I have the things I want. I don't see giving up, although people may not want a sixty-five-year-old hairdresser.

I don't know why but I never feel intimidated by anybody. I never feel that I'm not on somebody's level. Some of the nicer clients are often cleaners. That's the good thing about this job—you have a good mix of people who are duchesses or in the film or entertainment industry, along with office cleaners, plumbers—I like all that. The plumber from Sotheby's comes to me. And often sits next to the Duchess of Whatever. It can become very jolly, kind of like a big party. I love social interaction between my clients, you know, the club atmosphere.

You do have to remember when people ring up to speak to someone in the chair, if it's their husband or their lover on the phone and not get the two mixed up.

Most of the time it's a one-to-one—that's why people talk to their hairdressers, because they're a captive audience. Often you haven't even got eye contact so it's a safe, relaxed situation. It can be quite soporific. Sometimes people nod off.

If I think they're not very forthcoming—if I've summed up their personality—which you do get used to doing in five seconds flat—it makes me even more determined to make them warm toward me and want to continue coming to me . . . unless they have bad manners, or what I consider to be bad manners. Then I don't make any effort at all. But I can't remember the last time when I stood in front of the bathroom mirror, shaving and saying. "Oh no, so-and-so's coming today." I think that, without knowing it, I've weeded them out.

There was a diet guru who I couldn't stand. She wasn't just rude, she was bulimic. She'd plow through a bag of crisps and then go and stick her finger down her throat. She came twice and then there was an occasion where she didn't arrive for an appointment—it was quite late in the afternoon and she didn't arrive so I left and went home. And when she did arrive, a colleague of mine said, "I'm afraid he's gone home and to be perfectly honest with you, he doesn't really like you. He thinks you're appalling." And she said, "Oh—why didn't he tell me? I'd have understood."

In terms of becoming Nicholas's "dad," it wasn't a decision. I just grew into the role.

Sadly, the father wasn't interested at all in the child. My sister moved in with family when Nicholas was two, and my parents were so happy to take it on. My sister was a civil servant and she was working. So my mother would take him to school and bring him home and do all the feeding and washing and caring but my sister was always home for the bath and bedtime so she didn't miss out on that.

I think that children are very good at finding their father figure where they want it and I knew that Nicholas had found it when he came home from infant school with that first drawing: three stick people, him in the middle, holding hands with us, and above was written "Mummy, Me, Uncle." That's when I really realized that I had to take this role seriously and how important it was for me to be there for him because he decided I was the father figure. It's been a joy for me, mostly.

It was quite an unusual situation, the whole family under one roof, but Nicholas didn't think it was unusual because he didn't know anything else. It's not very British. My mother, sadly, died a few years ago but my father still lives with us.

Probably his fourth birthday he became aware his situation wasn't typical. He was sitting on the floor with a little girl and she said, "Where's your daddy, then?" And he didn't answer and she was rather a persistent child so she asked again,

"Where *is* your daddy?" so he said—and I overheard this—"I haven't got a daddy. I have an uncle," and that was the end of the conversation. She was quite satisfied with that.

I didn't do school meetings but we always had family holidays and I fell into the role—it's been a really important part of my life and I think I've gained a tremendous amount from it, being a bachelor and having no children of my own.

When Nicholas was very young, I lived with the family in Lewes and commuted to work. For the past eight years, I've lived in London Monday to Friday and gone home at weekends. Otherwise I'd have been missing so much.

That's why we never sent Nicholas to boarding school. Even with a weekly boarder, they come home and you say, "What happened this week?" And they say, "Oh, nothing much." And you've missed it.

Family meals are very important. Dinnertime. And Sunday lunch. Because that's when you have conversations with no distractions. And the preparation. Nicholas always cooked with us. If you don't want children to cut themselves with a knife, don't talk to them about it, show them how to use the knife. He started peeling vegetables when he was three. From the age of six, we'd give him a small glass of watered-down wine. At about the age of ten, he complained that the glass had more water than wine so we gave him a small glass. Now sometimes he has a glass of wine and sometimes he doesn't. Unlike some of his friends, there's no problem. I have a lot of European and Middle Eastern friends; I suppose that's influenced us. And our holidays are mostly in France—sometimes Spain or Italy.

My sexual orientation has never been discussed, because there's no need to discuss it. He's a very intelligent boy. He's perfectly aware of it. He's grown up with it. He's grown up with one or two of my friends whom he knows terribly well, including my long-term partner, who also has children of his own, and Nicholas is very close to him.

The house is always full of Nicholas's chums, and when I'd arrive from town, he'd always throw his arms around me and give me a kiss, never bothered whether his mates were there or not. When he was a university student, working at Tesco's for extra petrol money, I would wander into the store and he would always throw his arms around me. Nicholas is very sure of himself. He's very OK with the world. Interesting, isn't it?

Maybe it's because I've never been confused about my sexuality. I've never had a problem dealing with it and never had a problem with anybody else dealing with it. I just carry on the way I carry on. Even with my family—I never felt the need to discuss it.

I just always felt that Nicholas was actually very comfortable with other peoples' sexuality—always sure of himself enough to not have a problem. He's always been very into girls.

This is the first year he won't be on holiday with us. He has his girlfriend. And he has his head down, planning his career. I have a lot of contacts, so I can help him with that if he wants.

I remember saying—when he was twelve—I said, "If you want to see your father we are very happy to go out of our way to arrange it and you needn't feel you'd be letting us down in any way by wishing to because we completely understand."

And, frankly, I don't understand why he doesn't want to because if it were me, I'd certainly be curious. But he's shown no interest at all. He may well do one day. He's felt very secure. He's never felt vulnerable. Many of his friends are in similar situations, the parents split up and they don't see their fathers. I suppose you don't miss what you've never known.

His father remarried and has two sons, but he's divorced. It's a great shame that Nicholas doesn't know his two half brothers.

Once, when we were on holiday—Nicholas and I would go on holiday and spend ten days on our own before his mother or anybody else joined us—anyway, we sat on the beach and he said, "You know one thing I regret is that I have no brothers or sisters because the time may come when you and Mum are no longer around and I may very well be in a marriage or a partnership with children of my own and I wish there were someone who'd shared the same family experiences as me because it may be very lonely."

In some ways, my sister has taken on my mother's role for me, since my mother died. We didn't always get on. We squabbled like mad when we were young. But now we're very close and have the same taste in culture and the same opinions in politics. We have a very good time together and will probably end up like a brother and sister Darby and Joan. I always say to Nicholas, "You're not to tie yourself down to us in our old age but I do expect you to keep an eye on us, if only to make sure we have plenty of cheap sherry."

 PART 11

Fidel Castro's Filthy Nails

(*or* On Beauty Etiquette)

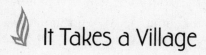 It Takes a Village

ROSE MCGOWAN

I am constantly shocked at how much money it costs to be
a girl. And how much time it takes. If I added up the time
I've spent applying makeup, removing makeup, getting my
hair and nails done, having facials, getting my teeth whitened,
having my clothes altered, and driving to these appointments,
I might want to shoot myself. It all sounds so incredibly triv-
ial. And yet, if my alternative is to be a hairy-underarmed,
Birkenstock-wearing, crystal "deodorant" user, I guess I shall
use the precious moments of my existence to not be a crunchy
person.

At work it's the pit stop crew. That's what I call between-
shot touch-ups. The hairdresser is teasing and pulling, makeup is spackling, on-set dresser is tugging, straightening, and
taping. The sound department is often running a microphone
wire under my shirt, and the dresser has to stick her hand up

my pants leg and pull it down to be plugged in. At this point the soundman is Velcro-ing what feels like an in-house arrest ankle brace that the sound wire plugs into. This all happens at once. I try to have an out-of-body experience while it's all going on because I loathe people touching me. When I'm in the makeup trailer, my nickname is MT for Moving Target. I get so bored and squirrelly. Nothing can be done fast enough.

In real life, there's still a pit stop crew, but it's at a granny pace.

It's completely uncomfortable when a practitioner spills her guts. There's nothing less relaxing than getting a massage by a girl who's asking how to become an actress because she thinks she's wasting her God-given talents by rubbing people.

I did Pilates a while back but stopped after realizing I'd been paying a ton of money for the pleasure of listening to my trainer's ongoing relationship woes.

I end up feeling bad that they're feeling bad and so my tip gets bigger. And then I find someone else.

When it comes to inexpensive versus expensive, the $8 manicure might not be as good, but I'm still not going to pay $50 for one. It's really $70 with tip, and that's silly. I have to save where I can! NYC is fantastic for cheapie blow-outs. Jean-Louis David is $25 for a rocking blow-dry that lasts. But I'd *never* scrimp on cuts, color, or facials. That's like a cheap bag. A no-no.

There are so many terribly tacky beauty trends. The brown lip liner with the frosty white insides. Very long fake nails with doodads hanging off. Flowers painted on toes. Crimped hair. Skunky highlights. Super-inflated lips. Cheekbone implants.

Bad hair plugs. Super-strong, overly sweet perfume. Let's not get me started on appalling fashion trends. That'd be a book!

I love the Golden Age of Hollywood, but I think it's unrealistic that women nowadays can spend the hours required to be perfectly groomed. Women were primarily housewives and were expected to look "presentable" for their men and make the time to do so. With the advent of women's lib, that well-coiffed era and all its trappings seemed archaic and something (understandably) to rise up against.

However, I think there is a middle ground to be discovered and reclaimed. Do I wish women (and men) didn't go around in sweatpants and making what looks to be a very concerted effort to look like hell? Yes. I don't think people have to look like glamour-pusses all the time, but making an effort is something I commend. I think it'd be hard to feel attractive, even to myself, if I wore sweatpants and scrunchies all the time. The bottom line is this: It's harder to be depressed with hot pink lipstick on.

My Body Will Always Remember You

JENNIFER BELLE

This year for Christmas, my father, my stepmother really, sent me a gift certificate for a massage at a place called Bliss Spa in SoHo. I bristled with anger when I opened the gift. I'd just had a baby via emergency C-section. I hadn't lain on my stomach in a year. The last thing I wanted to do was gallivant around a fancy dressing room in terry-cloth slippers, sit in a sauna, have my body touched by a stranger.

When I was twenty-one I got a massage once a week for forty bucks in a guy's loft in the Bowery. Looking back, I wonder what I had to be so tense about. Over the years I got massages sporadically, usually on my birthday, in a hotel, or a Chinese place on the street, or some scary basement somewhere with hockey puck Combats stuck to the walls, but now it was the last thing I wanted.

We had no college fund for the baby, not enough equipment, not enough help, and yet my father thought what I needed most for Christmas was a seventy-five-minute, $125 Blissage. When I called with my passive-aggressive thank-you—"And thanks for the massage. What a treat! I mean I'll have to hire a babysitter and try to find the time to go and we're so broke"—the message hadn't gotten through to him.

A year later, when the baby was one, I started working out again with my personal trainer, John Santiago. My back hurt from carrying the baby, and I longed to stare at the tattoos on his neck.

He was training to be an EMT—emergency medical technician—and he'd spent the day in the morgue at Bellevue assisting at an autopsy.

"How was it?" I asked. I knew if I could keep him talking I might be able to convince him to give me a stretch, something he'd only do if I'd earned it, which, my first day back since my C-section, I certainly hadn't.

"It was fantastic. I'd spend every day there if I could. But a strange thing happened," he said.

"What happened?" I asked, still lying on my back on the mat even though I'd stopped doing sit-ups several minutes earlier. I wished he would stretch me.

"I have this client, this girl who always comes in at six A.M."

"Jesus," I said. "Six A.M."

"Six A.M. Mondays, Wednesday, and Fridays. So when she came in on Friday, she was really freaked out because her roommate wasn't home when she left the house that morning. She said she always had to fight him for the bathroom, and it wasn't like him not to be there. Then when she came in on Monday, she said, she'd been so worried about him because she hadn't seen him all weekend but then, that morning, she got her boyfriend to open the roommate's door and poke his head in, you know, and the roommate was sound asleep in his bed, so she was really relieved. She figured he'd just changed his schedule or something."

"Can you stretch me?" I asked.

"OK," he said, "but just this once." He knelt next to me, holding the heel of my sneaker in his hand, and pushed my thigh excruciatingly into its socket. It was a reverse-stretch, more of a compression. "So then her place started to stink and it turned out her roommate'd been dead in his bed for three days."

I tried to focus on the pleasure of the stretch and the feeling of his hand grasping the back of my calf through my workout pants, instead of his disgusting story. "So then," he continued, "she said that she'd called 911 and the police had come and taken his body away to be autopsied, so I said, wait a minute, was he thirty-eight, with shoulder-length brown wavy hair and blue eyes? She said how did you know . . . and I said, *I autopsied him all day!*"

Something about the story, and the details that followed, made me think I should use my Bliss certificate right away, that day if possible. I should use it, feel my body, feel alive. It was just lying in a drawer, and for all I knew I could be lying in a drawer soon.

He was thirty-eight. Healthy. No drugs, no heart attack. No cause of death.

I called Bliss, and they said there'd been a cancellation and I could have an appointment that afternoon with Tony. When I got there, I checked in at a sort of phony reception desk, and was given flip-flops in a bag and a locker key like a camper. I didn't even carry a key to my own apartment—I hadn't locked my door in five years—and now I had to worry about this locker key. I had a baby to worry about, I couldn't also manage this key.

I tried to convince myself that putting on a strange robe and flip-flops was luxurious and I should be enjoying myself. I was shepherded into a waiting area where I sat on a couch next to a gigantic bowl of Gala apples. While I was waiting, I ate three, one after the other.

Tony, my massage therapist, came into the waiting room to collect me.

"Hi," he said, looking at me. "How are you?"

"I don't want much pressure on my lower back, but you can go very hard on my neck and shoulders. I had a C-section, so don't touch my stomach," I said. "I have carpal tunnel, bursitis, and tendonitis in both arms and arthritis in both hips and in my spine." I prattled on about my health problems, looking intently into his eyes. "I'd really rather not have creams or lotions put in my hair," I instructed. I'd just had it blow-dried straight. "I've been having a lot of headaches lately, I'm nursing so I can't take any medication. I really have a big knot right here." I tried to show him where the big knot was through the enormous robe.

"Anything else?" he said, smiling at me.

I looked into his wide warm face, thinking he seemed pleasant enough. Not creepy at all. He seemed a little blissed-out, but down-to-earth and handsome.

I followed him into the massage room and he waited outside while I took off the robe and lay down on the table, arranging the towel over me and my breasts under me for a few minutes.

I was starting to look forward to this. I just hoped he wouldn't talk. I didn't want to talk about my baby, or about my novels or about where I lived or anything. And I certainly didn't want to know anything about him.

"Ready?" he asked through the door. He came in and folded the sheet down, so my back was exposed.

Then he pressed his fingers into the middle of my back.

In an instant my year of massages came back to me. His loft on the Bowery, his wife and newborn baby in the next room, his shiatsu mat and meditation cushion. My body had remembered his touch.

"Tony?" I said. I twisted around to look up at him.

"I wondered when you would figure out it was me," he said.

It was my body who'd been the one to figure it out. Since I was twenty-one I'd had many massages and been touched by many men. I couldn't help but wonder if my back would remember every touch it had ever felt, like shoeprints in wet cement, if everyone's fingers had made as strong an impression, or if it was only Tony it would have remembered.

I just couldn't get over it. I'd sat in the waiting area, clutching my key and my apple cores, talking to him for ten minutes. I'd looked into his eyes, been told his name, heard his voice, answered his questions, but I simply hadn't remembered him until he'd touched me.

For the rest of the seventy-five minutes he massaged me the way he used to, and we reminisced. He was divorced, and I was married.

"I've gained weight since then," I said, cringing at the thought of it, and the list of ailments in my lament to him, and the scars from two surgeries. Since I'd last seen him I'd had an abortion, a miscarriage, and a baby. What did his fingers remember of my body? I wondered.

"It happens," he said. "You're still totally beautiful."

For the rest of the hour I was twenty-one again. My body was lighter, took up less space on the table. My hair was enormously big and curly, the bonding on my teeth was white and new, my arms didn't hurt at all. And my stomach! My stomach was round and smooth and untouched. I was perfect.

"My body was so relaxed back then," I said.

"What are you talking about? You had an ulcer. You were constipated. You had headaches and insomnia and TMJ, remember your jaw? Remember you had hives and eczema and you were constantly throwing up? You were just as tense right here." Again he touched the memory bank located between my shoulder blades.

He pressed his thumb into a painful spot along my spine he'd once told me was fear. I flinched.

I thought about my body one day lying on a table at the morgue. "You wouldn't believe what they do to you," John Santiago had said to me. "They cut you open like this." He traced a Y on my body that began on each shoulder and ended at my navel. "Then they take a scalpel and break each one of your ribs, the sound is incredible, crack, crack, crack. Then they scoop out all your organs, your intestines, your heart, your lungs, your ovaries, until you're completely empty so you see nothing but your spinal cord. Then they put everything they took out of you into a garbage bag if you haven't donated any of it. They put the Hefty bag with your organs in it back inside you and sew you up."

He'd put both his hands on my head.

"Then they saw open your skull from here to here and peel down your whole face and pull out your brain. They keep your brain too. They don't put your brain back in your head when they sew it up. I'm going to get to do more autopsies next week! I can't wait," he said.

I wondered if he would do mine one day. If he'd cut through the muscles he'd help me build. And I wondered if my body would somehow know it was he, be comforted by that, remember what it felt like to be touched by him and to be alive.

It seemed right for my trainer to do my autopsy, coach me through it, keep me strong. "It's supposed to hurt," he would say, "that means it's working." I needed John Santiago by my side. When I was pregnant, I'd wanted him to be with me in the delivery room. "I think my wife might wonder why you're calling *me*," he'd said.

"I'll tell you, it's a weird fucking way to meet somebody's roommate," John Santiago had said.

"It's a funny way to meet again, after all these years," Tony said.

I closed my eyes and let my body remember.

"You can turn over now," he said.

I turned over onto my back and he rearranged the towel. He pushed his fingers into my scalp, ruining my blow-dry. My back, my legs, my feet, my arms, my hands, my neck, my shoulders, my face. Even my hair remembered him.

ASA WRANGE
AND RACHEL STANDFORTH

Asa Wrange and Rachel Standforth met twelve years ago when Asa came to massage her. Asa was twenty-six and Rachel eighty-two. Rachel, born in Holland, was a teenage musical prodigy whose family was murdered by the Nazis. Her mother had managed to pay the Cuban consul to get Rachel out. He married her, taking her to Cuba, where she became a cabaret star. Rachel started from nothing for the second time in her life when she fled Cuba for America in 1960. Asa was nineteen when she came to America from Sweden as an au pair. Before becoming a chiropractor, she was a massage therapist. Massaging Rachel once a week, she gradually realized she was in the presence of the artist formerly known as Topsy Young. We'll start with Asa's story, because once you get to Rachel, a.k.a. Topsy, it's hard to break away.

ASA: I was very proud of the first massage table I had, and this was my first client I was going to, and I didn't know anything about him at all. He was in one of those high towers on La Cienega. I go there, and he opens the door, and he's a little Moroccan guy, naked, with a big gold chain around his neck! And he just said, "Hi" to me, grabs my hand, like, "Come in." I'm not really scared—I'm pretty nonjudgmental—but I'm like, "Oh . . . kay." And I walked in and set up my table—I'm trying to be professional, this is my first massage, right?

So he was naked, which was like, hmmm, but I was totally doing my thing professionally and everything was fine. But I couldn't get him to relax. Little did I know he was under FBI surveillance for the Heidi Fleiss thing. I had no idea until I left there and he gave me a beeper because he told me he was "the King of Beepers"! That was his claim to fame. He started Heidi Fleiss off, and he was involved with that whole thing.

He asked me if I'd consider massaging him in lingerie, and he'd buy it for me, but no, I wouldn't do it. He said, "I'll pay you double money," but no.

Then I had one guy that was way too loud and verbal—this guy who screamed when I touched him—but by then I had an office in a workplace, so that wasn't scary. I won't massage someone that overtly is trying to be sexual. I had this little Mexican guy that comes in. He likes to drop his pants and be naked. I can see that he's overtly trying to do something and that just freaks me out; I banned him.

Chiropractic is more effective than massage, but it's less intimate for most people. The thing is, when you massage people, when you go to someone's house, you're putting yourself in a completely different position. You are at their beck and call and at their mercy. I had one man who was a Parkinson's patient, very very wealthy man. He liked me to sit there and talk to him for an hour before I left so even if he pays me well for my massage I ended up spending two and a half hours there.

This is how Asa met Rachel, who remains one of her closest friends.

RACHEL: I'd met Swedish people before—I performed there, and in Finland, and all over Scandinavia. I've been all over Europe. I was in Russia, in Leningrad, I was in Germany, but that was before the war. I sing in seven languages, and I speak five. Straight away, I love Asa. She was so fun and also she was so sweet, she'd tell a lot of stories about her life, ya know? She was very comic, and she imitated men she knew.

ASA: I've told her everything. She knows about the strip bar I worked with when I moved to Los Angeles—she always says, "Tell me again about the man who said, 'Oosa, Oosa, what do you want from me?'!"

RACHEL: Everything, everything! I'm an open person. I have an orchestra, OK? And I conducted them when I was sixteen years old and had a fourteen-man band. I was in Paris for three years—I worked for Columbia Pictures, doing fifteen minutes of jazz before the movie.

My God, I had such a beautiful figure in that time, you know, I had some little boobies and very tight clothes, and I was very thin. One man, I was sitting with my aunt in a hotel having breakfast, and he was so beautiful—he looked better than Clark Gable! And he was so handsome and tall. I was blushing, because I was just a young girl.

My aunt got sick, she got a cold and she told my mother, "Look, I'd like to go back to Holland," which was around six hours by express train. She said, "I don't want to stay here anymore, I'm very sick. I have to leave the child alone." And my mother said, "Well, leave the child alone, she can take care of herself." So every morning I sit there, and that man is looking at me. Handsome man he was, beautiful dark suit, light silk shirt, a diamond on his pinkie, a big diamond! And he's looking at me and sending flowers to my table, and then after he asked the waiter if he could sit with me. And I was ashamed, for I was a girl just eighteen years old and I was all alone, my aunt had left. So I say, "OK, he can sit here. I don't know if my mother would like that though." I told my musicians, there's a man, I like him very much. And then he gave me a present: beautiful silver bracelets, and I didn't want to accept it. He said, "Don't worry, just put them on," and I said, "No no, I won't put them on."

He gave me perfume and purses and all kind of things that I didn't open! He said, "Look, I know some lady, she was a Dutch lady, and they have a restaurant." So we go there to that woman and we sit there, and she said, "Come to the kitchen, I'd like to talk to you in Dutch, so they can't understand what we're saying." So I go to the kitchen and she asked, "How can you go out with a man like him?" I said, "What kind of man is he?" "He is the biggest pimp of Paris," she said. "He has fifty-one women working for him!"

And he came to Holland and he said to my mother, "I'd like to marry her!" And my mother said, "Look, my daughter is not allowed to marry a man of your kind of work." He had a beard, he looked like he didn't sleep—he'd fallen in love with me! He was really . . . He went on his knees with my mother. And my mother said, "No way. My daughter cannot marry you."

Well, I left Holland nine months after Hitler. My whole family got killed—my mother and my brother, my father was dead already of a kidney infection. I met a Cuban who got me out, and then he got married to me. He was engaged in Cuba, but my mother gave him money to take me.

"Topsy" got a job as Maureen O'Hara's stand-in when Our Man in Havana *filmed in Cuba.*

RACHEL: Castro wasn't a Communist yet. When we finish the picture, in downtown Havana, Fidel Castro came and said to me, "Where you from?" I said, "I'm from Holland, but I'm a Cuban citizen." So he said, "Let me give you an embrace!" And he had such dirty nails. Disgusting! He smelled so bad. He became a Communist after that, and he threw the cross on the floor and stamped his feet on it. And his mother died from despair because she was a Catholic. Really! Castro's mother died of a broken heart.

Everyone was in Cuba at the time. Ava Gardner I knew. She was in The Capri, that was a nightclub in Cuba when I was making the movie with Maureen O'Hara. She was like a country woman, no makeup offscreen. She was just a round face and a little stout torso. Also, Rita Hayworth was there. She was very tall and skinny and she had very thin ankles. The most beautiful film face was Elizabeth Taylor. Her face, when she was young. But not her body. Her hands have very small fingers.

I never met Audrey Hepburn, but I never liked her. I always liked Joan Crawford very much, and Bette Davis. Those are the two. And then men, I like Edward G. Robinson. I worked with Errol Flynn. He wanted to take me to his yacht. And he didn't want to pay the bill. He invited all the entertainers in the club to the hotel, and he said, "Well, my presence should pay for it." He was so handsome. I didn't go to the yacht, though. Mainly, he liked a lot of black girls. He lived on the island too. He bought an island or something, and he lived there and he had a lot of sex with a lot of different women.

I always went to the hairdresser to have my hair and nails done. You know, when you make movies, they do it almost every day. They even changed my hair sometimes two times a day, the color of my hair! I think I have a picture as a blonde in my purse. Ask my daughter if I look good as a blonde. My own hair is naturally black or dark brown. I went red when I stood in for Maureen O'Hara. And it stayed.

Did women exercise then?
RACHEL: They danced a lot. The black bottom, and Charleston . . . all kinds of things.

Thinking back, she instantly transforms into Topsy, singing "La Vie En Rose." It's pretty. Then "All of Me." Mindblowing.

RACHEL: So I sing, all in feathers, when I go to Colombia. Josephine Baker sang after me—she was number fifteen, I was number fourteen. And she called me in her room, she said, "Miss Topsy, I have to talk to you. Miss Topsy, I am very sorry, you have to go to the middle of the show, number seven instead of number fourteen," because she came many times to Colombia, and the people knew her. But I was never there, so the people didn't let me go from the stage. I was too popular. Josephine was jealous. Beautiful legs, though!

Now the women they are too much about being thin, it's not beautiful. They don't look natural. You know, thin is OK, you know? But I don't like too thin. You have a lot of legs open here, so thin they are. It looks ugly.

In 1960 she fled Cuba for America.

RACHEL: They took everything away from me, my money, my jewelry, my clothes. I came with my daughter, she had one dress and I had one dress. Then I met my husband four years later, and he was such a lovely man and he never asked me for a kiss and I thought, *Maybe he's for the other side*, you know? But he respected me very much, and when he went back to Canada to fix the papers, he asked me to get married. And he sent me $400 every month to help me.

Having traveled the world, she came to believe very strongly in the power of massage.

RACHEL: One time somebody . . . he came by to massage me and he touched my fanny, and I gave him a big slap in his face! I always have women now do my massages. I had a woman, she was from Jamaica, and it was in Panama City. She only massaged my belly and that's where I find out it helps you lose weight.

ASA: So when I started, that was one of the things she wanted to make sure of—she wanted me to massage her belly because she had put on a little bit of weight on the belly.

RACHEL: But for ninety-one years, I don't look bad, right?

ASA: And you have so many different red wigs.

RACHEL: Yes, but my hair is also red under my wigs. I used to have gorgeous hair . . . thick and beautiful.

ASA: But when I first met you, your own hair was long and red.

RACHEL: It's still long!

Rachel suddenly announces:

RACHEL: She tells me all her secrets, but I've never told them to nobody.

ASA: It's true. Since I was very little, I've always been given to friendship with people all kinds of ages, and the age has never been an issue. And also, Rachel is super open. She's always said to me she doesn't feel a day older than twenty, on the inside. I think I am about . . . twenty-four.

RACHEL: I always talk to my daughter about Asa. Asa could have been a daughter. I love her like family. I was hurt, because many years I didn't hear from her.

ASA: That's me. I can be a little flaky at times, yes.

RACHEL: Yeah, well, you had your dog, and—

ASA: Yeah, but when I get all wrapped up in what I'm doing, I know that's bad, but she's been very forgiving about it, I must say.

RACHEL: Oh, I never get angry with her. How can you get angry with her? Beautiful girl like that. And sweet on top of it. But I would like to change all of Asa's clothes. She has shoes like a man, and they're always loose, she never ties them. But she's gorgeous, OK? She has beautiful boobies. You know, I could sing another little song for you?

JESSICA VARTOUGHIAN

Jessica Vartoughian is part of the vast Armenian community in L.A., and one of its biggest success stories. After coming to the United States in 1962, she opened the first nails-only salon in 1969. Nail salons did not exist beofre Jessica. In 1975 it moved to the space it still occupies on Sunset Plaza. Her oldest customer is ninety. Her youngest is her five-year-old granddaughter. Now a multimillionaire behind an international polish line, amazingly she attended beauty school in America before she could speak English.

Of course I was terrified, and I was very frustrated, because I like to talk. I like nails because I talk with my hands. You express yourself with your hands, so they're a key element of your whole . . . sense of yourself. But if you go to beauty school there are teachers that teach a general curriculum of hair or makeup, but there is no real specialty in nails. So I

found out myself, [so] that after only few weeks I was teaching the teacher how to give a manicure. I had clients who,
even though I didn't speak English, they asked for Jessica. I
used to get 25 cents tip or 50 cents tip, so that was my cigarette money and my lunch money or my bus money.

So, school was very frustrating and I failed twice. They
allow you to have a translator and the translator was late.
I lost my time, so I could not complete my essay. So, the
third time around I knew that book upside down. I mean I
knew that book with my eyes closed. So, of course I got my
license.

Now, when I go to my salon and I have my nails done, I
miss the doing the nails, being one on one with a client, and
make someone's hands beautiful. I enjoy that. And it's become
so big. I mean in England and Japan, I cornerstoned the market. There's a lot of working women, a lot of women who go
to work. And their appearance is very important. Having well-
groomed hair, not necessarily long nails—in fact that's out of
style—it's part of your security, you feel better, more secure,
and you talk with more confidence.

Before my salon, manicurists worked out of hairdressers.
I did not like to work with the hairdresser at all. I don't want
to follow anybody because you can't be creative to follow anybody. You have to be independent. So that's the first thing I
establish after I learn how to grow nails. It's just to establish
the environment.

When I go get my nails done, because I'm like practically a
client, it's one on one. Someone holds my hand, and cares for
me. And it's my time and I receive a loving care. Somebody's

touching me very gentle. I have some girls in my salon, two, three girls that are rough when they touch you. Not rough, it's a wrong word to say. They not . . . you know, it's like the way you move the hand, the way you touch the finger. They less tender with it. I have to talk to them about it.

Now, the part of my training was "Don't gossip with your customer." Just don't talk about other clients. We had a lot of movie stars, lot of wealthy people. Aaron Spelling with the kids. Tori was my client when she was five years old. So they were trained not to talk, at all. Not to ask questions. But to be very polite. To listen. To answer. To share with them who they are. When they were asked.

But I enjoy your salon because the women seem to be so outspoken. They're opinionated. I pick a color and they tell me I can't have it with my skin. I especially like X. She makes me laugh.

Hmm. For you, you like, it's your personality. It's just that . . . you have to understand your client. It's all psychological. Oh yeah it is. So I always understood my clients.

I made once mistake in my life. And I would never forget that mistake and I always repeat this to my girls and I tell them: When my daughter was born, I had very special clients, always, but there was three, four, you know, that they offer me their house when I do the baby's christening. So there was this lady who Vidal Sassoon bought the house after her. Not the one he's in now. The one on Canyon and Beverly Drive. So, she had a beautiful home, and more than the home was the incredible grounds. So, anyway, we have the christening there. A few years later she gave up her standing appointment for the week. All my customers had a standing. Four o'clock, three o'clock, two o'clock, whatever. So she didn't need that week because she say she had an important luncheon. Fine. So then she calls me back after a few days, "You know what, Jessica, the luncheon was canceled, and can I have my appointment back?"

I said, "I'm sorry, but I gave your appointment away for this time to Mrs. Reagan." At that time Mr. Reagan was the governor. Well, she was so offended, she never came back to my salon. You no idea how much hurt me that. I should have never say the name. You see, you learn.

Your "girls" have been working with you for a very long time, often many decades.

All of my girls have property, I'm very proud to say. Most of them are married. They have few divorce. They have money for plastic surgery.

Yes, one of your girls was telling me about her face-lift.

Only face-lift? Only?

What makes a good customer?

As long as their feet is clean. The customer who respects you, who comes in time, respects your timing, cancel in time. They aren't rude, because some people, very seldom, but they could be rude. But seldom, not often. I would say, in my career, I have maybe two or three customer like that.

She names a kittenish sixties sex symbol.

I did say, very politely, "I'm sorry, but you know you tried to humiliate me and you can't treat me like that. I'm just a person as you are. And I'm doing your nails and you have to treat me properly."

Do manicurists get carpal tunnel syndrome?

Oh yes. They do.

Migraines?

No. Because at Jessica we work with natural nails, so you don't have any odor or any of these bad chemicals.

I know in the salon you have Armenian, Romanian, Russian, one born in Greece. And we all get to have a cross-cultural exchange.

My daughter, Nadia was divorced for short time and funny thing is, now she's marrying an attorney who is a beautiful Iranian-Jewish boy. Which is great thing about America. She can marry anyone. Except a Turk.

I know the modern thing is to bring your little daughter for a manicure, but I wish the salon were adults only.

I agree with you totally. Except my granddaughter. She's a saint.

BEBE RUDU

Bebe Rudu, thirty-three, is a facialist at the ultra-exclusive Ole Henriksen spa in Hollywood. If she looks pretty enough to have been an actress, it's because she was, before she found her "calling." Her mom was also a facialist, back in Romania.

Eastern Europeans are famous for good skin care. I would go in after school and watch my mom work. I knew that I loved it, and I read everything there was about skin care out there, and my friends would ask me for advice. Pretty much everyone in my life was asking for advice about skin care, and I didn't know why because I'm like, hey, I don't do this for a living. I was studying something else—nutrition—and then I sort of walked away from that seven years ago.

Watching my mom, I saw how much she was loved, and how great she was and how beautiful the skin was after a fa-

cial, and I thought, *Oh my God, this actually really works*.
And then I thought, *I'm going to go get my license*. I had spots
on some shows and theater. I made a lot of money off commercials. But I had a knack for skin. It was a passion . . .

It took a year and a half to get the job here. I think I came
once a month to ask if they had any openings. For a straight
six months I kept on coming in here. And I think they got sick
of me and finally hired me.

What makes a successful facialist?

Well, I think people just love to be touched—it's all about
the touch. It's about touching and listening. I listen, and I
don't judge, and it's confidential—I'm not going to tell so-
and-so this famous person said this. We all love to gossip, but
when the door closes, it's confidential. I've spoken to a lot of
aestheticians and massage people and they're like, yeah, it's
like we have something between us and the clients with the
unspoken words.

I mean, I'm not their psychiatrist, I just kind of listen and
maybe share the situations I've been into, maybe my life's
situations.

Has anyone ever told you too much?

It wasn't ever to the point where it was, like, too intimate.
But I've had too much, energy wise. I tell you, sometimes I
feel heavy. I've picked up everything that's going on. Sometimes, without even knowing, I get a feeling that there's
something going on with my client, and then they start telling
me or they start crying. I've had women just all of a sudden

cry in my hands. I think I may have hurt them, was it the extraction? But really it's something else going on and then they start opening up to me. And sometimes it's happened on the first time I've ever seen someone. It's actually happened recently—I had a girl cry on my table because she had a hard time with her skin, and the funny thing was she was gorgeous.

Sometimes *I* find myself telling them things and I'm like, Oh my God, I don't even know this person! And I'm telling them things more than I have my best friend! And that's why when I was watching my mom, I saw these relationships go on and on and on for ten, fifteen years, and I was amazed how much my mom cared for these people. One time she had this woman who died—she was older, and she started with her older—and my mom just cried and cried for weeks and I just thought, *Oh my God, this is her client!* They became so close, but she never was invited to the Christmas dinners or the birthday parties, she just had that relationship with her at work.

I have told people things I haven't even told my best friends or my mother. I've told things to my clients because I do feel safe too. And of course you can get in trouble because you're talking and they know the person! They're like, Oh really? You're engaged to *him*?

How do men react to having a pretty lady do their extraction? Are you asked out a lot? Are they embarrassed?

Yeah, I've been asked out, yeah. I mean, not a lot, and it's interesting how men actually go there, and I think it's because of the touching and they feel like, Oh . . . wow. I don't think the first time they come, they're like, Oh let's go out, like I'm going to say yes—I've never gone out with a client before because I've always been in a relationship. But they take their time and . . . it's normal, because you know celebrities always marry the makeup artists. And there are so many out there that were actually massage therapists. So a lot of celebrities, actually, end up marrying the aesthetician or the therapist, ya know? When it comes to celebrities, we're not like someone out there saying, "Oh my God there's Keanu Reeves," or "There's Jennifer Lopez." When they're here, they don't feel like we want to get something from them—we're actually fixing them and they look up to us. So then they feel safe. And that's why I think a lot of men start liking that person because they feel safe.

I have some celebrities that have a hard time the first time. They say, "Oh, I've heard you're good," but then I put the light on them, you can tell they're cringing. They have such a hard time and I have to stop and say, "Listen, I see eight faces a day. Look at me like I'm a doctor, there's no judgment here." And they're fine, but it's true that some of them think, *She's gonna judge my skin, I'm not so fantastic without my makeup on.*

I care about my clients and I really, really want to fix the skin, it's not just applying lotions and masks and letting them just kind of sit there. I understand because the world out there, it's so hard already in Hollywood . . . the women over forty, you know how it is. They don't feel as youthful anymore so they're trying to do everything, so I understand that it's very sensitive when your skin looks horrible. I understand that.

Do you do your own skin?

I have this thing, it's weird, like, everyone trusts me to do their facial and I don't trust other people. Everyone here is fantastic, don't get me wrong—but yeah, it goes to the same thing. I have a problem with people touching my skin.

In the Makeup Chair

INDIRA VARMA AND ANITA GIBSON

Indian/Swiss actress Indira Varma was raised in England, where she was plucked from drama school to star in Mira Nair's Kama Sutra *at nineteen. She later became a muse to Harold Pinter, who originated several stage roles for her. Last year she made a splash in HBO's* Rome. *Sometimes the shortest-lived shows lead to the deepest friendships. It was on the set of the speedily canceled medical drama* 3 Lbs *that she worked with Anita Gibson, the first makeup artist who she says truly understands ethnic skin. Although makeup for black, Asian, and Latin skin has finally become a boom industry, there are still very few black makeup artists. Anita, who works most frequently with Spike Lee, is at the top of her field. Indira interviewed Anita as she made her up for a six A.M. shoot in Queens, New York.*

INDIRA: Is this what you wanted to be when you were a kid?
ANITA: It is not at all what I wanted to be. I actually wanted to be a fashion designer, when I was a child. Then I discov-

ered that I didn't want to do the design as much as I wanted
to do the market for design. So I came to New York, to go
to school for fashion marketing, called the Toby Colvern,
which was affiliated with NYU. After I graduated, my first
job was with Victoria's Secret. Being the overachiever that
I was when I was young, I moved up the ranks very quickly.
I managed my own store on Madison Avenue within eight
months. And discovered I was a slave for no money. But
I was young, in New York City, and it was exciting. I was
being invited to all these parties with celebrities and music
people. So I decided I didn't want to do that anymore. I
wanted to enjoy my life a little bit. One of my coworkers
was moving on to Estee Lauder. And she said, "You should
come with me, you'll make more money. And you won't
have to work as hard."

INDIRA: So you based your career and work around your social life?

ANITA: Absolutely! That's how you have fun! So I went to Estee Lauder. And just started doing makeup. And I found
out that you make more money, just by putting makeup on
these women, because they buy more products from you.

INDIRA: Did you always know how to do makeup?

ANITA: I always fooled around with makeup. Growing up
I was always looking in the mirror. Putting a full face on,
and then just staring at myself. Never really going anywhere . . .

INDIRA: What age was this?

ANITA: Probably around twelve.

INDIRA: And your parents were cool with that?

ANITA: Yes, totally. I mean I didn't go out with it. I would just put it on and stare. I used my mom's makeup and my sister's makeup. And they would yell and scream at me.

And my mom's white, so I couldn't put on her white face makeup.

INDIRA: Is your sister a lot older than you?

INDIRA: She's just three years older. It was perfect. She was going out with her face all made up. And after she'd leave I'd pull all the makeup out again, play around, and just stare at myself, wowing about how I changed.

INDIRA: How long were you at Estee Lauder?

ANITA: Probably about three months. Because the account executive was moving to Yves Saint Laurent. And so she said, "I'd love for you to come and do makeup with us. And work on our industrial commercials, and do all these kind of things . . ." So I went off with her, and then from there I started doing fashion shows. Yves Saint Laurent was much bigger than Estee Lauder.

INDIRA: But did they do any tests, or train you in any way?

ANITA: They would send you to the little school for their company. But it's actually more about their products than actually teaching you how to do it. I was very good in art. So the artist in me created the makeup artist in me.

INDIRA: And you learned just by doing it on women?

ANITA: Absolutely. And I got better and better. "If I make her look great, I'll be able to pay my rent sooner." And back then, that's all it was about. Paying my rent, buying all the latest fashion, and being able to go into a club and have a good time.

INDIRA: I don't associate Estee Lauder with black make-up . . . ?

ANITA: Oh no, not at all. And Yves Saint Laurent surprisingly only has two caramel-y foundation colors. But their bronzers, eyes shadows, and lipsticks are all triple pigmented, which is perfect for women of color.

INDIRA: What does triple pigmented mean?

ANITA: It's just a higher density of color. Less titanium dioxide. So when you have more pigment, it's going to show up stronger, but it doesn't move as well.

INDIRA: What is titanium?

ANITA: It's white, basically. If you read the ingredients of any color makeup, if titanium is listed high, that means it's gonna go ashy on black skin. If it's listed way deeper, it means the color is going to be true on a darker-colored skin tone.

INDIRA: How come you know all of this stuff?

ANITA: I was actually going to start my own cosmetic line, so I worked with a lot of chemists, and I did start the line, and we were ready to go into Barneys, but last minute, our investors backed out. Barneys was all set up, we had our counters, it was terrible. I do understand what their point was. The climate had changed. There was a time when you were going into Barneys and *then* you branch out. Now because of all the J-Los and Jessica Simpsons, and all these kinds of people coming into the business at the mass-market end, and *then* going high end . . . now you don't have to go high end, and then mass market. So they just weren't going to get a return on their investment fast enough. And everything is about how fast you can get their money back to them. So we really had to rethink what we were doing.

INDIRA: Then you were asked to do catwalk?

ANITA: Yes, then I was doing fashion shows. Which allows you much more creative freedom. It also teaches you how to do it really fast and where you can cheat. You're getting your girls that are coming from a totally different show, with all their makeup on, and moving and flexing them into an entire different mold.

INDIRA: Having worked on the counter where you're dealing with woman of all ages, all ethnicities, all beauties . . . or not . . . is it hard to transition to *models*?

ANITA: Yes. That's what had been special to me and still is: when I could make a woman who didn't think highly of herself look in the mirror and say, "Oh my gosh, oh my gosh!" I knew I was good. That is a very difficult task. If you can make a woman feel good about herself, even if she can't repeat it at home, it was satisfying. With models, some of them aren't very nice. They really don't care, it's more "Hurry up so we can get these clothes on and walk." But they're just doing their job.

INDIRA: What came after catwalk . . . ?

ANITA: Then I started going into the stores. Because catwalk is seasonal. You only get two pops at it. And you need back-up income. So I started freelancing with Bobbi Brown, Yves Saint Laurent, Chanel, and went back to department stores. Getting better and better and better, because in the store you're constantly applying makeup.

INDIRA: So when did you get into movies and television?

ANITA: Everything just drops in your lap when it's destiny. My girlfriend was doing a film. And they needed a makeup artist. And she was going to L.A., so she couldn't do the first two weekends. And they were filming for three weekends. And I told her, "Oh, I'll do it for you, it's no problem." And that's how I got into film. That movie was kind of geared around hip-hop music and black culture. From there I met Russell Simmons, Chris Rock, and so many people from the music industry. So I started doing tons of music videos, and working with a lot of celebrities. And that's where I really took off.

INDIRA: I know that you mentioned before that there just are not many black makeup artists. . .

ANITA: Oh no, there are hardly any. But now, coming up there are probably a lot more. Especially out there, people that aren't in our union and doing film, there are hopefully a lot more women of color doing makeup. But in our union there are only a handful doing this . . . and doing this well. It's sad because it's just so hard to crack into this business. And then for me, I'm very much across the board. I'm not doing just black makeup, or just black projects. I do all projects. That's real success. I'm very lucky.

INDIRA: I know this may seem a little far-fetched. But do you think because you are mixed race, so you've had experience with your mom, and her skin, and also your own skin . . . do you think it's had an impact?

ANITA: I definitely think so. I think not even so much the skin, so to speak—more the experience. My mother is white, and so I'm used to being around white people, functioning around them. And then being around black people, and functioning around them, and then just coming into my place of work, and making everyone comfortable. I know when I can let a little bit more of my black flavor show through. You just have to sit back and feel out the vibe. Some black people don't know how to do that. Some people are only giving their black flavor. And white people can be very intimidated. Amazingly, people sometimes have no experience at all with black people, or black culture. Which is very sad to me. But you know, that's how life is. So I always know, I sit everyone in my chair and, as my one girlfriend calls it, I do my crossover Negro thing. Making them very comfortable. Enunciating everything. By talking to them, I feel out if they have had black experience. Whether it's through a friend, or through work. Then I can let loose a little bit. And have fun. And it's definitely a side of me that's very funny and you have a good time with it.

INDIRA: Have you ever witnessed people being intimidated?

ANITA: Oh yes. Of course. And I can pick that up before I even bring that out.

INDIRA: How did you manage to become not just a "black makeup artist"?

ANITA: Honestly, through star request. When a star requests you and only you to do their makeup.

I was Linda Fiorentino's makeup artist, and Natasha Richardson's. They wrapped their arms around me and just kind of brought me along too.

INDIRA: Do you still want to start up your own makeup line?

ANITA: Yes, because there is still such a void for quality make-up for women of color. There's more things coming out, but while the white women's makeup lines are saturated, we're still so limited in our choices.

INDIRA: Who do you think makes the best makeup for women of color?

ANITA: A line called Naomi Simms had the best foundation. Where is she now? If you're out there, Naomi . . . come back!

INDIRA: What kind of people do you like sitting in your chair?

ANITA: I like smart people that can talk about all kinds of things. I appreciate everyone, but I particularly enjoy people who can have a conversation about anything, or have knowledge about things I do not.

INDIRA: Do you think men are more vain than women?

ANITA: A lot of men, definitely.

INDIRA: What do you think makes a good makeup artist for TV and film?

ANITA: Well, the high-definition TVs are changing everything. With film you can sneak away with a lot. Whereas HD would tell on you right away. Makeup artists definitely have to be on top of their game.

INDIRA: Do you think that means that actors like me, if I don't have great skin, I'm going to find myself unemployed?

ANITA: No. Good skin doesn't override an actor's talent.

INDIRA: Does the camera really add ten pounds?

ANITA: Yes. Yes it does. I do shading to minimize these effects. Especially in the face. Body shading is looong and tedious.

INDIRA: Is it true that a lot of actors marry their makeup artists?

ANITA: Mmm no. But a lot of them sleep with them!

INDIRA: Are there any people that you think don't need makeup at all?

ANITA: No! Everybody needs a little something.

PART III

Fix Me

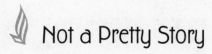 Not a Pretty Story

FRANCESCA LIA BLOCK

I am a pretty writer. In spite of my college creative writing teacher's warnings, I am an adjective queen. I can produce descriptions of warm, smooth, soft, burnished, suntan-oil-scented skin that may satisfy my loneliest reader's need to touch and be touched. I create faces, using imagery from flowers. I write about food in such a way as to make your mouth water. The foods are all things I can't eat because of my sensitive digestive system, so my descriptions are fueled by my hunger for vicarious pleasure—zingy diamond-pale champagne from a black bottle; aphrodisiac, orgasmic chocolate; pastries stuffed with cream; brews of rum, lime, soda, sugar, and mint that make you tingle with an alcoholic's longing. My books are filled with scents to bring back lost days: raindrops sizzling on the dirty pavement—an August downpour in L.A. when I delivered a rose to a man who didn't want to sleep with me; vanilla oil activated by a dancing stranger's sweat—my tall, blond, high-cheekboned cowboy rock star darling, Fred, who died of AIDS after fighting it for almost twenty years; the fragrance of pink peonies—a windy, sun-dappled city spring and my personal resurrection after my father's death from cancer.

I am a pretty writer. That is to say I can write pretty stories, not that I am pretty. Even if I were pretty I would never write such a thing. How crass it would sound! But I can comfortably say that I write prettily. I developed this talent because I did not feel pretty, and if you weren't going to fall in love with my face, maybe you'd fall in love with my words.

What you are about to read is not a pretty story. It is not written to make you fall in love with me, at least not in the usual way that I try to achieve this. It is written to expose the unpretty truth. I won't lie and say that I have outgrown the need to have you appreciate me; maybe this will connect me to you in a different way.

This is a story about a relationship with someone who touched the inside of my face but it starts with someone who intimately touched the inside of my mind. Neither mind nor face felt pretty before, or after.

I chose both touchers poorly.

My therapist said to me, "What exactly don't you like about the way you look?" She asked me about each feature. "Do you like your hair? Your eyes? Your mouth?" I told her that I didn't like my nose. It had a bump on the bridge from when I was about six; my friend's cute older brother collided into me in the hallway with his toy gun. My nose bled profusely;

no one took me to the doctor. It wasn't a good model for my future—boy you like hurts you (accidentally) with (toy) weapon, you cry, bleed, it hurts, no one takes care of you.

I also didn't like my skin. I had acne scars as well as deep lines around my eyes and general sun damage from frying on the beach without sunscreen as a teenager, partly as a way to sear away the offending acne.

"I know a plastic surgeon," the therapist said. "We can go as one of your sessions." She also told me that she herself was considering plastic surgery and wanted to see what his work was like. I did not think I was being used as her guinea pig, but even if I had been conscious enough to see this, I would have gone ahead. Finally someone was guiding me toward a solution. Maybe surgery would not only straighten my nose and smooth my skin; maybe it would help me find a way to love myself.

So I went with the therapist to see an extremely handsome, tall, sleepy-eyed man who spoke softly to me and told me I was already pretty. A man who potentially had the power to make me pretty and who told me I was pretty to begin with—a dangerous thing. He also showed me a photograph of a blond woman with a nose that had been badly twisted by another plastic surgeon. My handsome surgeon had corrected this, and the woman was now lovely. I was sold. I gave him all the money from my book advances, signed away his responsibility for my accidental death, closed my eyes and fell into a magical sleep from which I hoped to awaken transformed.

The plastic surgeon removed the fat beneath my eyes. He said it would make me look younger. I was in my thirties at the time. I need that eye fat now. My eyes look sunken and hollowed out. They look less like my five-year-old daughter's beautiful eyes than they would have if he had not touched them.

The plastic surgeon used lasers to remove the top layer of skin on my face. I blistered for almost two weeks. The heat in my body was almost unbearable. I took Vicodin every few hours. My mom applied ice packs and fed me ice-cold drinks through a straw. When the blisters healed and the flaming red color faded, my skin was smoother. I still have acne scars around my mouth. My eye lines came back in a few months. I also got something new—brown spots and generally uneven pigmentation around my jawline from the peel.

The plastic surgeon removed part of the bump on my nose. There was still a noticeable bump. It is hard for me to imagine how a professional cosmetic surgeon could cut open someone's nose at the tip, peel back the skin, shave down the very bone, and not achieve a straight line. He also resculpted the rounded tip using cartilage from inside my nose. He created an exaggerated squared-off tip with one uneven nostril.

I disliked my face so much before that I was actually happy with these results. At the time, they seemed better to me than what I started with. Plus I was enamored with the surgeon. My therapist kept encouraging me, emphasizing that she knew he was still single. During my recovery he came to my house and picked me up in his sports car. He drove me to his office and removed the packing from inside my nose. A man who can fix your face (I hadn't yet seen the results) and pick you up in a sexy car, in your pajamas. Very, very dangerous.

Eventually I called my therapist to tell her that every time I came in to see her I tried to bring up angry feelings I had toward her, that it was very difficult to do in person, and could we address this in the next session. She yelled at me, "How dare you say that. After all I have done for you. You are an inhumane person." When I confronted her in her office she apologized and explained that she had just received the news that a friend had died. I said I understood but that I wouldn't be able to see her anymore.

I went on to marry, have two children, and eventually separate from my husband. I didn't have much time to think about my face. Mostly I just gazed, dazed with love, into the exquisite perfection of my babies' faces. Except one night, during a horrible fight with my husband (I am ashamed to admit it had to do with the *Sports Illustrated* swimsuit issue), I looked at myself, bloated, red, distorted with pain and tears. The sight was shocking. I looked the way I felt inside.

Sometime later, I went out with a man who said to me, while we were in an intimate position, "There are women who are more attractive to me but this is better because you won't be as much of a distraction." What is most worrisome about this is not that he said it, but that I continued to see him for some time after.

Shortly following this, the *New York Times* came to take my picture for an article. The published photograph was a brutally close shot of my face. I saw with shock the way the cartilage in my nose seemed to have slipped, leaving a sharp point sticking out on one side. The tip of the nose was swollen and leaned off to the left more than before. I just hadn't wanted to look at this but now there was no mistaking it—my mis-shapen central feature was blown up on a page of the *Times* for all to see. I should have been happy about the attention the article would bring to my work but I felt literally sick to my stomach.

These two events brought me back into the office of the handsome plastic surgeon. He was much less charming than the first time I had seen him. He reached across his big desk, took my nose between his thumb and forefinger and pinched it. I heard him say these words, "I really made it lean over to the left, didn't I?" When I wrote to him later, asking for some financial aid with corrective surgery, he denied that he said this. Maybe he said, "It really leans over to the left, doesn't it?" I was in a state of shock and could have misheard him. I do know that I asked if he could help me and he said, "You are very thin-skinned. Not like me, I have thick skin. Your skin would scar. I'd be worried about going in again." I asked what else he could do for me. He suggested Kenalog injec-tions, steroids to make the tip appear smaller and less swollen. He wasn't sure if it would work but we could start that day. Wary of steroids, I said I'd have to think about all this. Luck-ily I waited because I was told by another surgeon that the injections would have exacerbated the problem—reducing the surrounding tissue to expose the uneven cartilage. The first surgeon also suggested taking fat from my abdomen and injecting it into the lines on the side of my mouth. But he warned me that if I suddenly gained a lot of weight, the fat in my face, thinking it was still abdominal fat, would swell grossly. I told him I wasn't interested in this now.

I have had my nose redone by two surgeons. It was a four-hour-long operation, and much of it was spent repairing the gouged-out insides of my sinuses that had been practically destroyed by the first surgery. My nose is far from perfect. The bump is gone and the tip is smaller, rounder, more natural, and almost symmetrical. At a party a plastic surgeon's wife gave me a lecture on how her husband could improve my nose, though she did say, "At least you have a straight one now." I get fewer sinus infections but my sense of smell has been compromised. I haven't even let myself think about how sad it is that I will never have the sensual and mnemonic enrichment of this sense in the same way again. I've had more (painful) laser therapy to improve the discoloration along my jaw line. It's still there and I plan to get another treatment. My eyes are still a bit sunken-looking and will continue to get more so over time without the cushion of stolen fat.

Still, generally, I like my face much more than in the past. I think finally it looks like mine. And inside, I feel like it. Tired, sad, aging, but also expressive and giving.

Recently I was discussing *The Wizard of Oz* with a friend. She told me that the wicked witch frightened, but mostly fascinated her; that she admired her much more than Glinda, the good witch. I said that I disliked the wicked witch because the way she looked was how I felt I looked. My friend's response to this startled me into a new awareness of the extreme quality of my belief. That was the image I carried of myself—green, warted, hook-nosed, pointy-chinned. I remember the boy I had a crush on in junior high telling me that I'd be cute if someone cut off my head. I remember running down the street after my father told me his cancer had come back. Some boys in a car whistled at me from behind. When they saw my face, wracked with pain, they screamed, "Ugly!" so loudly that it still echoes in my mind. No wonder I put myself into the hands of the surgeon and the hands of the therapist. I would have done anything to try to become Glinda-pretty.

These days, the only hands that touch my face, besides my own and my facialist's, are those of my beloved five-year-old daughter and three-year-old son. Nothing feels as sweet as when they put their fingers to my cheeks, to my eyelids, to my lips. I never used to let anyone touch my nose in the past and now I welcome their caresses. After the surgery, when my daughter first saw the dark purple bruises on my face from the hours of hammering, she told me what a pretty color the marks were. In her eyes and her brother's, I am beautiful, at least most of the time. In their hands, I am safe. With them, for them, I will continue to heal.

Will my pretty writing ever be the same? Maybe not. The description of scents certainly won't be as powerful. But maybe I don't need to make you fall in love with beauty anymore. Maybe I can touch you with the truth.

JANE AND JOY

It's nine P.M. *on Halloween 2006 and Joy Gorman is waiting for her toenails to dry. Gorman, thirty-three, is a Hollywood manager of directors and writers at Anonymous Content. Her life is a whirl of film festivals, deal making, and studio smackdowns. Her BlackBerry is constantly buzzing. The only time she is not reachable is when she's at Jane Diu's having a pedicure. The store is tiny (7216½ Melrose Avenue). Prices are low—$10 manicure and $12 pedi. There are only two chairs at Melrose Nails. It opened two years ago, and Joy has been coming religiously after walking in off the street a year ago. Two months back, a huge, fancy nail salon opened across the street. It sits there like a Texan mega-church. Joy has made it her mission to keep Jane's business alive.*

JOY: I cried when the place across the street opened.

JANE: It's very mean. I don't know why they do that. My customer they say, "Oh, that's mean!"

JOY: That was really scary for Jane.

JANE: My clients stay with me, they say, "Oh Jane we love you." Joy, she come back with me every week. I know Joy and she always comes back. If she leave town, she call me.

JOY: One time I was in N.Y. during a crazy work week and Jane left me a message.

JANE: Oh, ya. I didn't see her. I worry about her.

JOY: "Joy, where are you, Joy? I miss you! OK, love you!"

Did your boys dress up for Halloween?

JANE: Tonight the little one is the green Power Ranger. My big boy is very good student. He bring me certificate, he say, "Mom, see I make you happy!" I worry about my son because I work here late. He say, "Mom, do you love me?" I say, "Yeah I love you!" He say, "I love you, Mom!" I say, "If you love me you have to do good job in school."

I live with my mother-in-law. I love her. She love me too. Sometimes I think that she doesn't love me because I work a lot.

Where did you work before you opened this shop?

JANE: Big place. Thirty people. Too many. In Santa Monica. Beverly Hills. Laguna Beach. They make me feel bad. "Go faster!" I'm not enjoy manicure at all. I cannot stay. They always bother me, everywhere.

JOY: They made her rush! Jane has a pride in her work the way I do. She just would rather take a long time and make it perfect than rush to have more customers, and that's why people come back to her and they wait for her. People don't do that in this town.

JANE: A lot of customer say, "She do good job!" After that they fire me. I think maybe they are jealous.

Joy, your mom died a few years back. Do you now find yourself drawn to the energy of older women?

JOY: Yes. Jane always says, "You miss your mommy today, Joy." She's looking out for me.

JANE: Yeah. I tell her that. When she came in I love her right away. She like a little girl.

JOY: That's why no boys will marry me. I always tell you, "Look for my husband."

JANE: Last time, you remember the man?

JOY: Who hit on me while his girlfriend was here?

JANE: Ya. He gave me the number and he told me I give you.

JOY: He turns to me while she walks out and says, "How do you tell your girlfriend when her outfit's terrible?" And I said, "You don't." So not relaxing.

Do you have other friends here from Vietnam?

JANE: I have best friend, I came to USA and she come too. She live in Oregon with her husband.

What does she do?

JANE: She does nails.

What did she do?

JANE: She was an accountant.

What did you do?

JANE: I was a schoolteacher.

Were you afraid to come to America and start again?

JANE: I speak little English so I feel bad and I was scared of nails. My mother-in-law wanted me to go to nail school. I didn't want. I never done it for somebody. I was very afraid to cut cuticle. My hand would shake. Every night I go home to Buddha and cry, "Please help me cut cuticles I am so afraid. I want to do a good job!"

JOY: She'll never tell anyone she's closed. She'll stay here un-til eleven-thirty at night. My little time when I come to see Jane is very sacred to me. Nothing more annoying than paying for something that's supposed to make you relax and going to someone who doesn't give a shit. It really matters that she cares, about her work and about me. If I go to yoga and I deserve a treat, I'd rather come here than get frozen yogurt. I walk in and she says, "You look so good, Joy, you're so beautiful."

I started looking into Buddhism recently, and I think Jane is Buddhism in action. Jane has a lot of faith. If you can feel that in somebody, it's so special. My dad said to me once, "You were raised in chaos, that's comfort to you." Coming here is my solace because I have to sit down for two hours. I do a lot of work here. I always come with a couple of scripts. I have friends come sit with me here.

I'm very protective of Jane. If I send a friend here and they don't get it, that's a problem for me. One friend said something negative and fangs came out.

When I was away and Jane called me in New York and told me she loved me . . . it made me really sad. Because I think she thought that I had left her. But I would never.

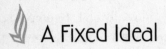 A Fixed Ideal

EMMA FORREST

I was ending it with my fiancé and I needed to talk to someone. Even if my shrink had been able to squeeze me in, I don't think I could have faced the summer subway ride all the way up to Ninety-sixth Street. Searching for a substitute stranger I could pay to hear me vent, I walked around the corner to the hairdresser. Someone—if not a shrink, it could have been a manicurist, facialist, or bikini waxer. My neurosis and me, we were wed. I just wanted us to look *good* together.

The hairdresser's was the closest—and I was able to march in and get a blow-out. But the stylist was gay and bitchy instead of gay and nurturing and just not interested enough in me to ask about anything other than *who* had done my color. He didn't ask about my love life and, unprodded, I didn't tattle.

Post-blow-out, my hair was a strange combination of

straight and damaged, which was *me*. Nondrinker, nonsmok-
er, no drugs. And so I had to be creative in expressing the
damage. Bad choices in love was the major way. Men who
could hurt me. Men I could hurt by letting them see how
much they'd hurt me. A cycle cycling faster and faster until it
was a blur I could walk through and out of unnoticed. Once I
fell out of love I could never conjure it back. In my head, the
men I broke up with had all been aliens who died on the way
back to their home planets.

Since I couldn't manage it romantically, I looked constantly
to my appearance to make things stay a fixed ideal. I was especially envious of women with signature dos—but the more I
tried for one, the more I kept changing. In search of my signature, my hair had been pink, purple, honey, platinum, black,
red, streaked like Anne Bancroft in *The Graduate*, buzz cut
like Winona, then grown out to a Louise Brooks bob.

My weight fluctuated too: Jessica Rabbit curvy, Doris from
Fame zaftig, *Flashdance* lean. In summer my skin was Latina
dark, in winter it was shtetl pale. I realized as I walked home
from the hairdresser that the only constants on my body were
my tattoos.

The Vargas girl panther was a crazy first tattoo. It had taken
three hours to do and spread across my entire right shoulder.
It wasn't planned. I was eighteen, killing time, bored, waiting
for the friend I was vacationing with to meet me for dinner.
"Who wants to tattoo me?" I had asked, walking randomly
into one of the many parlors on Hollywood Boulevard, and
the answer was Baby Ray, a big, frightening-looking man with
a shaved head. In my manic swing I just happened to have

gotten lucky, as, unbeknownst to me, Baby Ray was a famous artist people traveled miles to see. A lovelorn loon, he, of course, took to me straight away:

"Baby girl, I'd marry you in tennis shoes."

I didn't know what that meant but I accepted the compliment, and as he sketched his design for my shoulder, he begged some more.

"Please let me, please let me . . ."

I had heard that somewhere before, but it wouldn't click until after the tattoo was finished and he dismissed me coldly for the next girl. A rite of passage through gritted teeth. Stumbling out of the room pale, silent, and bleeding. Why would I ever do it again? Only a psychopath would do it again.

Five tattoos later, my straight and damaged hair still warm from the blow-dryer, I searched my cupboards for a number I had tucked away. The blow-out had been so unfulfilling; where was that number? I found it in my freezer, where I stashed my financial documents (the desk drawers being overstuffed with unpaid bills). I called Tom, though I had been warned he'd be booked months in advance. Beautiful women of New York, across the ethnic board, had tattoos by him, a connecting factor I hadn't failed to notice. I went to a friend's sample sale with my mother weeks earlier and as we looked around my mum asked, "Have you noticed something? They're *all* thin. All size two."

These brittle women, Tom had had them all, and the softest thing on their rock-hard bodies was always his tattoo. I dialed the number on the card.

"This is Emma. I'm a friend of Tina's. I know you must be

booked solid today but I thought you might have had a cancellation and I'd just check to see . . ."

He interrupted me, in a voice soft as the inside of a rabbit's ear.

"Come by."

He hung up. Suddenly I had the will to walk through blazing heat, garbage stinking, as it should around a dirty girl with five tattoos. Five tattoos by four different men, what a slut!

As soon as I saw him, I knew the inside of his ears would feel as soft as a rabbit's. Tattooing a 9/11 tribute onto the thick arm of a firefighter, he was thin and pale, so pale I sensed the blood moving under his skin. Combined with the little round spectacles perched halfway down his long, bony nose, the pallor gave him the air of a Talmudic scholar. The receptionist, Bettie Page bangs and Bettie herself rendered on each arm, led me back to him. He paused and smiled at me over his glasses—I saw his blue eyes smile before his lips. I smiled back, feeling a calm seep through me like ink. He had relatively few tattoos for an artist, the most prominent one a tribal design creeping up his neck. His light brown hair stretched down to it. I thought of trapeze artists, reaching for one another.

Behind him were his inks, photos of a pretty, skinny woman I took to be a girlfriend, and a shelf of little wooden sculptures. Following my stare, he said, "I whittle things. As a hobby."

I wanted him to whittle me. Into a different shape. Thin enough to be his type.

"Can you tattoo me? Now?"

He paused, tattoo gun in the air. It seemed to float in front of him like a kite.

"No. I don't do that. Even if I had an appointment free, I wouldn't do it. If you wait we can talk through what you want. Then I need you to go away and think about this."

He sounded like my psychiatrist, to whom I hadn't had the will to journey. I couldn't remember what it was I had wanted to talk about in the first place. The guy I was supposed to marry? Oh, he was nothing next to Tom. I waited for him to finish, excitement pulsing through me.

In the waiting room he sat down across from me, and I passed him the illustration from "La Chauve-Souris Dorée" by Edward Gorey.

"Edward Gorey!' His eyes lit up like the neon ink that had just come onto the tattoo market.

"I've always wanted to do a Gorey. I'm amazed no one's asked for one before."

He looked at me as if I were a wrapped gift. He studied the drawing some more.

"Where do you want it?"

I lifted my shirt to show my lower back. Spotting the foot of my Vargas girl cat, he lifted my shirt higher. He frowned.

"Whoever did this shouldn't have gone so deep. They didn't need to. They should have been a lot more gentle with you."

I took the first appointment he could give me. But before we left, we talked about how he had come to this for a living. He was a skinny, white art nerd at a tough, all-Mexican school. The aspiring gang kids forced him to tattoo them. He was terrified. Then we talked about his pastimes—chess and Buddhism. The Buddhist Tattooist. By the time I got home he had started to shape the lover in my book *Cherries in the*

Snow. Where my boyfriend was failing to inspire the character, he was filling it in.

I looked at the Gorey drawing of the vampire ballerina.
Though the image, long desired, would not be on impulse,
the placement was, and it was decided when I saw Tom.
I asked him to put it on my lower back, where it would
cover my last tattoo: my boyfriend's name. I had gotten it
at one of the myriad salons on the Sunset Strip, instructing
the artist, "Make this very faint. I don't know that it's going
to last."

It was a short name. It took a short time and didn't hurt.
Tom on my mind, it took a short time to break up with him that
night, and that didn't hurt either. Besides, I reasoned, though
he was devastated, I would be paying penance through pain
when I underwent the cover-up.

Friday came and the shop was finishing for the night. Tom
waited for everyone to go. The receptionist gave me a backward glance as she left. He locked the door and turned the
sign to "Closed." In my memory we dimmed the lights but I
know that we didn't because he needed it bright, with his bad,
Talmudic eyesight.

"What do you want to listen to?" he asked as he mixed his
paints.

We settled on Johnny Cash.

"I hurt myself today/to see if I still feel."

He arranged me on a chair that faced backward, cabaret
style, and tucked my T-shirt into the snaps of my bra. He put
his hands on my back, and I felt like I would melt but hoped
his hand would melt into me instead, so I'd be filled with his

strange, calm spirit. But his hand stayed solid, bringing with
it the whirring needle.

"You ready?"

One thousand jolts a minute, dipping in and out of ink,
then in and out of skin. I said mantras in my head, "Mama
Mama Mama," who hates tattoos, could barely look at them.
"Papa Papa," who gets so upset when he sees mine he has to
walk out of the room. "I love you I love you," someone, anyone. It seemed to take forever but I didn't want it to be over
because then I would have to pay and leave. I wrote poems in
my head. I miraculously remembered the words to the prayer
for atonement. In Hebrew. Me: the Jew with the tattoos, unable to be buried in a Jewish cemetery. The Jew disrespecting
those who had been tattooed *by force*. The Jew who had loved
only Gentiles.

Afterward we admired our work together, like lovers mar-
veling over a shared orgasm. Then Tom noticed something
that made him frown. We had failed to cover the dot in the "i"
of my ex-boyfriend's name.

"I'm sorry, Emma."

I wasn't.

"Well. I guess I'll have to come back."

I skipped home. I was so happy. I *loved* my tattoo. It had
been done by someone who actually gave a shit whether I
lived or died. Life life life. That's what I wanted. I was on fire
for weeks. He had given me his e-mail. But he never checked
it, too busy with chess rallies and meditation. Besides, with
the magical, psychopathic "unsend" button AOL provides, I
took back everything I told him I felt. Words were removable.

The ink, ancient, dating back to Polynesia, wasn't. Tatou: Hawaiian for "to hit repeatedly." He had me knocked out.

I needed to see him again.

I came back to Tom with an idea that we cover the "i" with ballerina slippers falling around the vampire dancer's head. That was a dumb idea because they're bigger than her head, and honestly, it looked a lot better before. No one can ever tell what they are or put them in context, and that's my fault, not his, because he kept saying, "Are you sure?" and I said yes because I was sure I wanted to spend more time with him. And this was the best excuse I could think of.

The slippers were bright red and looked diabolical, satanic. They frightened me. I was too troubled by them to fantasize about Tom. I wanted him to fix it. A week later I went back and he changed them, with the addition of white ink, from a red to a pink. They still look odd. On my author picture for *Cherries*, in which I face backward on a chair as Tom had positioned me, you can see the feet and legs and bottom of her wings, the parts of the tattoo I like. The ballet slippers when I went over the top because I just wanted to be around him, I made sure they were obscured by my T-shirt.

As we went back and forth each Friday night, trying to perfect the tattoo, Tom gave me little glimpses into his life—which I craved, but also resisted, because it meant hearing about the woman in the photos above his table.

"When you do this job, day in day out," he told me late one night, the shop, as ever, closed, "you have to have an understanding partner at home. Because the sensuality of working so closely with skin carries home with you. It can be hard to shake."

Still, I stretched our time to as many sessions as I possibly could. I'd rush home to write before the tattoo healed and dried over, so inspired by him, this man who knew how to make a needle feel gentle.

Somewhere along the line I even introduced him to my mother. It seemed important somehow.

"This is my mum. This is Tom."

He looked up from his work and smiled, that beatific angel smile, better suited to a John Cusack hero than someone drawing blood from a Puerto Rican.

"I can't be in here," Mum said and dashed outside for air. But: "He has a wonderful face. A *good* face. I can see that."

By then the tattoo had gone as far as it could. The vampire ballerina a testament to his expert hand, the falling ballet slippers a testament to my impulsivity disorder. I had to make excuses to drop by. I was just passing through the neighborhood, which I mainly was. Only I usually wouldn't take such great care to wear lip gloss and mascara on a run to the health food store. He always seemed happy to see me. If he was working on someone, he'd pause. If the tattooing chair was free, he'd make me sit in it as we chatted and shared coffee. He told me he'd broken up with his girlfriend. That he was glad to have an ear to spill to. And then he let me be on my way.

I passed Tom's number to one of my best friends. She wanted me to be there for support when she had her dead cat's name inked beneath her ribs. I felt odd as I watched them together. It broke something of a spell for me as I saw her fall under his spell too, the anesthesia of his smile, just as I had done.

At a party that weekend I met a New Zealander new to the city, and I had my first great sex. It was not frightening or tooth gritting, bringing up all the bad memories of the first time. It was amazing. He stayed in the city and we fell in love. He said he had been reticent about me at first because he heard me talk about the Buddhist Tattooist.

"I thought you were already in love."

"No, no," I protested, "Tom is just my tattoo artist!"

We'd felt like we'd last forever. But we didn't. In time the vibrant love broke down and disintegrated.

Of course, I never told him that I had seen Tom, once, outside the tattoo parlor. I had run into him by happenstance, walking home from a concert. He had been out with his co-workers and his breath smelled of whiskey. We kissed, outside a bar on Thompson Street, late at night in the rain, long after the tattoo had totally healed. Though he is very handsome I thought of "Chelsea Hotel," Leonard Cohen's song for Janis Joplin.

"We are ugly but we have the music."

I thought of it because of what Tom does for a living and what I do to myself. Of what I *used to do to myself*, before I met him.

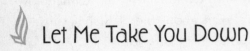

Let Me Take You Down

BARBARA HALL

My family was the biggest disappointment of my father's life.

The reason I know this is because he once said to me and my sister, "This family is the biggest disappointment of my life."

We were teenagers, which is a perfect time to hear that kind of information. I was starting to have acne and bad posture, while my sister was skinny with protruding teeth and a curious problem with chewing things. I seem to recall digesting the information rather matter-of-factly. It made sense when I compared us to the Ashworths, who had a boat and went to the lake every weekend, or the Criders next door, who had a trampoline and frequent outdoor barbecues. Clearly these people were happy to be seen in public. We tended to stay in the rec room a lot and watch television. Once a week we did trot ourselves out to church for a public exhibition, all dressed in finery and, in my mind, linking arms. My mother, a former model, knew how to dress us and we looked pretty spiffy but it was a fragile holograph.

Before the sweeping declaration, he had only cherry-picked things. My sister's lack of coordination. My mother's swearing. My smart mouth—smart not being an asset here. The lack of cleanliness and organization across the board. The fact that we never invited his mother to dinner. We left lights on. We didn't have the right friends. The list was endless and meaningless because it really had nothing to do with us. It had to do with the prison of his own mind which kept him in a perpetual state of victimhood. We were the visual components of that. We were his tragic energy transformed into matter.

I didn't get that at thirteen.

Here are a few of the things my father told me: I would always have to watch my weight. I had no grace. I was a smart ass. I was stubborn. I was arrogant. I had no common sense. I wasn't afraid of the devil. I was too loud. I was a tomboy. And many, many versions of me projecting slut energy, which was inconsistent with the tomboy concern, but we are not mining for logic here. It was a disconnected, disorganized, constant static in the house and in my head. My father was disappointed.

When it came time to find my very own man to let down, the garden-variety American boy wouldn't do. I had to go to England to find one who looked like a Beatle, went to Oxford, spoke the Queen's English. Someone whose entire heritage made mine look like a pound puppy. He adored me at first, then started finding little chinks in the armor. My decorating

taste was bad, much of my wardrobe "didn't suit." He mim-
icked my French accent when I tried to speak it and told me to
fermez my *bouche*. He was appalled at the gaps in my knowledge concerning British monarchs. He was equally disturbed
that I didn't know the Monty Python Philosopher's Song by
heart. He quizzed me on both. No, I mean, he quizzed me on
both. I think it was my inability to differentiate two obscure
Russian composers that ultimately caused him to declare me
a "cultural lemon." What a pronouncement! That could keep
me busy for a lifetime. And it would have too, if he hadn't
gone and found someone more culturally citrus.

I eventually tired of working out this dynamic in my relationships. No one could ever live up to a man who was disappointed in my entire ancestry dating back to the Druids. Fortunately I lived in Los Angeles, where along with someone to
read your dog's mind and whisper to your baby, you could pay
a guy to be disappointed in you.

I met the kung fu master at my daughter's karate school. I
saw him break a coconut with what seemed like a mere flick
of his wrist and I thought, *Whatever that is, I want me some
of it*. When I signed up for private lessons, I warned him that
nothing in my past suggested I would have any talent for
breaking solid objects. He shrugged and said, "Anyone who
tries to learn this is going to look retarded at first."

I was thrilled. Not even my father had ever called me retarded.

The kung fu master was cute, with zero body fat and ridiculous muscles. He was an ageless-looking nice Jewish boy
from Bronx Science with a Catholic name (we'll say Patrick)

and a genius IQ. He looked a lot like my first grown-up boy-friend, but this wasn't why I was attracted to him. It was that condescending smile, not condescending in any obvious way, and which could have been Jungian projection on my part, but the point was, it was going to be difficult to catch him at contempt.

After all, martial arts are about enlightenment, not Dr. Phil–style self-improvement, and the ultimate goal is to ac-cept yourself as a perfect extension of Source. That's what he said, anyway. He said lots of fancy things I didn't quite buy. Probably the hardest-to-swallow paradox of kung fu is that on your path to transcending the physical plane and becom-ing one with Source, you are taught how to crush a human trachea.

The first couple of lessons, as I anticipated, were new age-y gentle complete with a Buddha bar soundtrack. Even though I was indeed retarded—I think I actually injured myself in a standing meditation—he refused to correct me with harsh language or show any sign of condemnation. He just smiled and breathed into his belly and told me that there was no right and wrong. No right and wrong? What the hell? Wasn't my money as good as anyone's? This was George Bush's America. Don't try to sell me no right and wrong.

Week after week I was certain the tolerant smile took the place of an exaggerated eye roll, tugging at his willpower like an ancient desire to smoke. But no matter how much my cuts and punches sucked, I couldn't break him.

Like any man whose affection I was attempting to hunt down and kill, he got me to do things I didn't want to do. In addition to being a world-class coconut mangler, Patrick was also a medical intuitive, so for no extra charge he scanned my body and found that I was starving for enzymes. Somehow Source forgot to put these enzymes in any naturally occurring food, so they could only be obtained in the form of bullet-sized pills.

I told him of my snooty disdain for drugs, which was really a lifelong fear of choking.

"These aren't drugs," he said. "They are nutrients."

So he taught me how to swallow anything smaller than a Cadillac by breathing and shifting my beliefs.

Then he got me to give up wine. I knew he thought consuming alcohol was up there with consuming human blood (and in my religion it is but we don't say that like it's a bad thing), so I left empty Cabernet bottles lying around and waited for him to scold me. He didn't. Instead he lovingly suggested that I could try going without it for a while just to see how I felt.

I don't know if I felt that much better. I just know I enjoyed covering my glass at dinner parties and saying I was abstaining per my kung fu master's instruction.

"You do kung fu?" people would ask, impressed, and I'd say, oh yes, even though I was aware I still couldn't punch a hole in wet paper.

I kept sucking at kung fu and he kept being fine with it, so I thrashed around for ways to make him see me. My usual default position—sarcastic wit—worked on him, but in a way that didn't quite satisfy. Patrick responded to humor with a perfectly straight face and an intense declaration of "That's funny." After six months I had yet hear to him laugh. I had fantasies of throwing him down and tickling him until he screamed.

I kept swallowing pills that made me nauseous and not drinking wine and doing wall sits and breathing into my belly and dreading every lesson and not being able to break it off. I knew if I could gently lift up the top of his skull I would find a big puddle of disdain.

The truth finally came out one afternoon when he was teaching me to hone my meditation skills. He was explaining (again) that the point of life was the connection to Source.

I said, "OK, but how do you connect to Source on an airplane?"

I'm not really afraid to fly, but every time I fly, I manufacture that fear because like a lot of people, I find fear to be a real enervating force. Getting on a plane has the potential to be dreadfully boring unless you can conjure an abject terror, and then have that terror relieved by a Bloody Mary or eight.

"The plane isn't real," he told me.

"It feels pretty real," I said.

He shook his head. "Only your connection to Source is real."

I said, "But what about the people? You're surrounded by all those angry rude people and their bad energy and ugly clothes. The people are real."

He shook his head again and said, "Other people don't really exist for me."

A look crossed his face; he heard himself. I heard him too.

He readjusted and modified his statement to include his students and his girlfriend but it was too late.

I didn't exist.

This was hands-down the greatest version of rejection I had ever encountered.

What to do with it? Was that better than disappointment? The same as? A whole new pursuit for me, like realizing there was another dimension? Whatever it was, I was sure that now we were cooking with gas.

This kind of self-obliteration was what I had been after all the time. Patrick could have told me that. He was the one who had explained during our first session that the entire quest on Earth is only to be seen and recognized and validated. It's the only way we know we are real. He was saying this as an argument against such a quest. That we needed to free ourselves from such a base desire, otherwise we could not know Source. He had achieved this. I had not. His soul had entered some divine MySpace and I was still bumping around in the Earth plane trying to get someone to like my shoes.

Instead of upping the ante, though, I suddenly and mysteriously lost interest. I stopped calling him. I got busy at work, I went out of town, I met a man for whom I did exist.

This man, who had blue eyes and a normal amount of body fat, became important to me for several reasons. One is that he mocked the kung fu teacher. "Sounds like he just needs to go to Fatburger or something," he said. Another is that he made me laugh, really hard, seventh-grade laughter that gets you in trouble with the teacher or, in our case, the people sitting next to us in fancy restaurants. And I noticed that after one evening of laughing that way, I felt as if I'd slept for a week while hooked up to a wheatgrass and spinach drip. I felt high, the good kind, impenetrable and immortal. Way better than a standing meditation and no injuries.

The best thing about this man, though, was that he had a condition with a long name which meant that he couldn't remember people's faces. They just didn't register on his retinas the way other things did. He could remember voices, not just their sound quality, but their colors. He said mine was yellow with flecks of paprika; that was when I sang. When I talked the paprika was more pronounced.

He had so much trouble remembering my face, especially my eyes, that he wrote notes to himself like an Alzheimer's victim. The note he wrote about my eyes, which he put on a Post-it on his computer, was "Worth it."

The kung fu master left indifferent messages at first, just his name and number. Then he started being all kind and solicitous. He was worried about me. He wondered how I was doing. He was concerned about why he hadn't heard from me. He was there for me whenever I wanted to start working again. For some reason, I had begun to exist for him.

I e-mailed and said I was taking the summer off, I'd think about resuming in the fall. He wrote back and said that was just fine, whatever I wanted.

My father used to tell me that I was his idea, not realizing that I could and did interpret that to mean my mother didn't want me. But that wasn't really what he was trying to say. He meant that I was a thought bubble over his head, and when I dared to rearrange the contents, he felt betrayed.

When I was twenty-five I made a fever-pitch effort to get him to be impressed by me. It was, I think, the last time I consciously tried. I had earned a little money in my first job so I put together a trip to Europe for myself. I was going alone and I was fearlessly going to march across the continent that my father had always wanted to see for himself. To my face he was pleased and interested. Behind my back, to my sister, he shook his head sadly and said, "She never used to want to see the world."

Every time I breathed I hurt him. Because I reminded him that I was not his breath. I don't know if it was his job to fix that or mine to understand and rise above it. What we did instead was sever the connection. We weren't talking when he died.

Three days later I saw him in a dream. He was being escorted by some kind of spirit guide and he was looking around the house I lived in, which he had never seen before. Then he went and looked at the office where I worked. He was nodding as he surveyed the surroundings. It wasn't that he approved; it was that he could see I was all right. And I could see the same about him.

I don't care how many standing meditations you do and how many enzymes you swallow, I don't believe we ever transcend our connections to people. Nor should we aspire to. When we cash in our molecules I guess anything goes but here in the Earth school we are shackled. We leave impressions on each other that won't wash off, even if it's just a voice, vapor trails of yellow and paprika. We are tied together like orphans to a rope so that even in the dark we can feel the tug and no one gets lost.

The Chi Gong Show: My Year of Healing with Master X

LAREN STOVER

Picture this. The acupuncturist who has been overseeing my chi gong practice has a New Year's banquet celebration at the Chinatown Holiday Inn. He will dance with a long sword. But he forgets the sword and must improvise. He dazzles us instead with a long stem rose. He is agile, strong, yet ethereal. He embodies both masculine power and poetic prowess—yin and yang. The rose is whipped around, slicing through the air. His movements are improvisational yet the dance has perfect flow. I expect to see swirls of light spinning from his chakras. I forget that there is nothing at the $50-per-person banquet I can eat because I am a gluten-intolerant vegetarian and don't eat deep-fried anything or breaded meat. I don't particularly mind that there is nothing that I can drink since they ran out of tea and there is only Pepsi. Dr. X says that when your energy is right, you can eat anything.

Despite all the swirling around, none of the petals fall off the rose.

Dr. X was going to save me.

My friend Kenny had been raving about Dr. X for years. I was hoping acupuncture could cure fibroids.

"The guy cures cancer," he says, "but it's hard to get an appointment."

By the time I go to see Dr. X it is not for fibroids. I had a newly diagnosed condition. I have a mammotome biopsy followed by a lumpectomy. The post-op protocol? Six weeks of radiation, five days a week. Something like five or eight percent chance or better odds there will not be a reoccurrence. I interview radiologists at Sloan-Kettering, Cornell and St. Vincent's. They are all gung-ho—piece of cake—but I'd read that if a single cell is damaged by radiation and not killed it could start a new cancer; that radiation can fracture ribs, cause pneumonia. Many women who submitted to radiation did not die of breast cancer, but some did die, instead, of heart disease, and my tissue had been scooped out of my left side. Radiation would radiate the heart.

I go to Gilda's Club on Tuesdays, at my lunch hour, to meditate. I meet a woman who says, "I had what you did. I did radiation. Within three years I had invasive cancer of both breasts and had a double mastectomy." She must have been sent by my guardian angel.

* * *

Dr. X's office is in Chinatown. He doesn't close the door during the consultation and doesn't ask me to close it. I get the feeling that closing the door is, in fact, not allowed. As we discuss my pathology report, my medical diagnosis wings its terms out of the door into other rooms. Strangers in the little rooms next to me know more about my health than my friends. Even my sobbing is public. He doesn't tell me he will heal me but I sense he approves of my decision not to do radiation. He tells me I am responsible for healing myself.

"If you cut off a breast you won't get into heaven," he tells me. "You have to have all your body parts."

This is harsh news, but many spiritual teachers offer challenges to evoke emotions, to test strength. Fortunately, I pass the test to continue seeing him. And fortunately, I have nearly all of me intact. With his guidance I would reach the health jackpot.

Later he says, "If you noticed I did not close the door. The universe has no secrets."

This seemed an inevitable truth. I had found someone who could listen to the cosmos. And share its wisdom.

He guides me into a large room divided by gray curtains and I lay face up while he stings needles into me.

I look forward to my visits. I ask questions. I tell him my dreams. He treats all information with equal gravity and flippancy. I don't always understand his answers—but he, and TCM (traditional Chinese medicine), are going to save me. I can feel it.

On my fifth consultation, Dr. X advises me to do a standing

position with knees slightly bent, eyes closed and arms ex-
tended as if hugging a tree or holding a large ball, instructing
me to "do this two hours a day." He tells me to do this with
my husband. "If nothing else," he says, "at least you will both
be very healthy."

Two hours a day? It looks ridiculous. I can barely sit still for
five minutes to meditate or do creative visualizations. "I can't
do that," I say.

After that, he refuses to see me again. Pawns me off onto
the other acupuncturist. I am devastated. I want Dr. X to take
my pulse and critique my tongue. I want Dr. X's magical energy to vibrate through his hands and into the needles that were
aligning my energy. I'd found my ideal healer with excellent
credentials: handsome, adorable, contrary, intense, earthy,
spiritual, otherworldly, a consultant at a prestigious university
and born on Valentine's Day. And I'd been dumped.

I asked the receptionist why he won't see me. "He decided
her energy was better for you. She's sweet and he's sour." I see
his associate. Her needles hurt even more. She tells me it will
take a long, long time to heal my kidney energy. I need to go
twice a week.

The only way I can see Dr. X again is to sign up for his
breast-cancer workshop.

We are led by a student teacher; we stand in a circle in
front of our chairs and do some gentle exercises; it ends with
us "holding the ball." There seems to be no way out of this
"holding-the-ball" thing. How long, I wonder, am I going to
have to stand here with my eyes closed? Is anyone peeking,
watching the clock or seeing how silly we look? What do I

look like in this position, anyway? Is my stomach sticking out? I am too superstitious and obedient to peek. I follow the rules, especially Dr. X's rules. Minutes pass, maybe five, or ten. Dr. X comes out and tells us to stop. When I open my eyes I see, standing across from me, a tall, beautifully boned woman with a feline beauty, Tania, the interior decorator. She looks as uncomfortable with all this as I am.

Dr. X is holding healing retreats for patients. People from both his New York and New Jersey offices; people with weight issues, cancer, anxiety, you name it.

"What's it like?" I ask the student teacher. The student teacher has beautiful eyes. She has a beautiful smile. And beautiful energy. I envision a cozy sort of Zendo, rice-colored walls and Dr. X's special tea in a cast iron pot on the floor near the futon. "It's like sleep-away camp," she says. "Like the girl scouts."

Camp? Was she kidding? I find the whole idea of camp, any kind of camp, to be vile. I'm not the sleeping-bag type. I can't sleep on foam pillows or sheets with even the smallest percentage of polyester. Ride in a car with strangers? And sleep in a room full of strangers? No way, José.

But there are things you'll do . . . if you trust someone . . . to save your life. And Dr. X would be our healing guru for three days. I was "shifting my energy." Opening up. Changing.

Tania and I sit captive in the back seat, stopping when our driver and her friend, cheerful, beautiful people, possibly in the weight-loss program, stop at Dunkin' Donuts.

(Remember . . . when your energy is right, you can eat anything) while Tania and I bond over my organic almond, walnut and raisin mix and her Turkish-date-almond confection.

All the rooms sleep twenty people in bunk beds but Tania and I claim an intimate room with five twin beds, two of which are taken by over-bleached, oversized women who are in Dr. X's weight loss program. They snore all night, their whale-like girths gently swelling in the moonlight, peroxide tresses gleaming. The other cancer patient in our room, an ethereal, gentle brunette, clamps on a headset, but Tania, bald from chemotherapy, and I spasm with suppressed laughter. (Thanks to Tania I have started seeing her magical oncologist, Dr. G, who teaches us meditations and gives us millions of supplements.) Eventually, I take a sleeping pill and am reprimanded for missing the 7:00 a.m. meditation. Seven a.m.? I might get up that early if there was a fire, but not on a weekend. Not after the snoring lullaby of my roommates. But I would change. I would feel compassion for the whale ladies. And I would talk to them, something I never would have done a few months ago. I suggest they let us go to sleep first. Dr. X is changing me already.

All day Dr. X lectures. We learn about the seasons, the five elements, healing mushrooms (only wild-picked are potent), the Tao. He makes a soup. It is the best soup I'd ever had. I write down the recipe. Next he sautés watermelon rind. Everything he serves is healing. I feel his chi enlighten my cells, giving them a new energy. My cells are going to be moving to a higher vibration . . . I take notes. Dr. X reads childlike stories with profound, cryptic meanings. Later, Tania and I are singled out and given a gift of this book . . . cartoons inspired by a major Daoist text. It becomes my daily inspiration.

That night the bleached whales, exhausted from the day's events, hit the beds early. They snore again. I take more pills. I am sleep-deprived but delirious with energy and joy. They are spiritual obstacles, teachers that the universe is providing.

"Everything," says Dr. X, "is fate. There are no accidents." He lectures on TCM for three days. We hold the ball . . . I am beginning to feel something. His advice to many questions was to "Let it go." In other words, don't worry.

Back in New York I buy his book, his tape, his teas. Everything he touches has a sort of shimmering energy. He even designs the labels on the bottles of Chinese herbs he and the other acupuncturists prescribe each visit. They are images of crop circles.

Tania and I want to study chi gong at the Center. You have to apply and write a paper that Dr. X reviews. It's a more nerve-wracking test than the SAT.

I write the paper. I'm accepted. I'm ecstatic. So is Tania. We buy chi outfits from Dr. X. Baggy T-shirt and tai-chi pants, puffy shapeless things with elastic at the ankles. We do not tell them what size we prefer, we simply take what they hand us. When we get a look at ourselves in the large mirror at the Center, Tania says maybe we should be consultants on the redesign of the outfits and then we realize in a flash, that the plainness is probably meant to promote humility, and that this one element of our lives is not about glamour or chic. Every Tuesday evening I go to class. I meet a woman named Sally who practices while wearing a snug pearl necklace. She wears the pearls like a talisman, as if it's not jewelry at all but powerful gemstones. She'd had a rare form of cancer that meant she

needed a bone biopsy once a year. We're all looking for healing and leave our fashionable shoes and cashmere sweaters in
the dressing room.

Dr. X doesn't teach the level-one students himself but he
materializes at the end each night to "test our energy" while
we "hold the ball"—Tania peeked and saw him circling around
us like a mouse sniffing cheese. I try to empty my mind of all
thoughts but I wonder if my energy is passing muster under
the chi-scrutiny of Dr. X. I happily write a check for the classes and sign a paper promising I will never study with anyone
else. I agree to pay $100 if I leave the class and then come
back. Why would I leave?

Sometimes Dr. X plays the piano while we hold the ball.

"You play the piano, too?" I ask in awe.

"I don't play the piano, it plays me," he quips, and it's true.
No Chopin or Beethoven, no Elton John was he. Not even
Phil Glass. He twinged out tunes that shattered my concentration, and sent discordant shivers through me but I thought,
it's okay. Stop judging. That's the old you. His energy is healing, ignore the discomfort. Who needs harmony?

He began to sell tapes of his "healing music." All the students buy them.

I have stopped eating dairy. I have stopped wearing nail
polish and underwire bras. I have stopped drinking coffee.
I have let go of my prestigious window seat in the creative
department at work to move further away from the toxic
paint and spray-mount fumes. (Dr. G says these toxins bio-
accumulate in breast tissue.) But the biggest habit I have to
let go of is worry.

"Let it go," Dr. X advises me.

But what about this and this and this? "Let it go."

Let it go becomes my mantra. Holding the ball becomes the most important thing I do each day. As I hold the ball I start to worry that I won't catch a cab at 8:15 in the morning for an appointment days away. I learn to dissolve the concern. The cabs come and I always arrive at my destination in record time. Suddenly, I am always on time. Sally, like me, observes that since practicing, elevator doors magically open before she summons them. I find that strangers smile at me. My intuition blossoms. I stop getting colds. I feel strange physical sensations in my body that Dr. X explains is the energy going where it needs to go to heal. He tells us not to try to guide the energy. Just "let it go." It feels as if my energy is aligning with the external world. Sometimes I feel the chi moving me, like a water hyacinth in turbulent water, or a reed in the wind.

Dr. X has a full-moon meditation. We sit quietly, but not for long. Behind me, a guy barks. Someone else grunts. Another person breathes strangely.

"I think some students have Tourette's syndrome," I tell my friend Tania. Why would they try to disturb other people's peace on purpose, it has to be Tourette's.

The next week in class Tania says, "Those were the advanced students. They've had their channels opened."

"But it bugs me," I say. "It's rude."

"Let it go," Tania admonishes.

The advanced students practice after our class. They so adore Dr. X, whom they call Master X, that they often take up collections for him and expect us to chip in, too. They de-

liver his newsletters at six A.M. before they go to their jobs.
They mop the floor on their hands and knees, sweeping damp
rags devoutly over the linoleum with determined expressions.
They clean the plants, spraying and polishing each leaf.

I don't feel any urge to clean, but then, I am not advanced.
I have not had my channels opened.

Finally, conveniently in time for the next chi weekend, Dr.
X finds a few of us ready to graduate.

I feel as though I've won a Pulitzer. A year of steady practice—thirty to forty-five minutes a day—paid off.

When I see Ron, a psychic healer, I tell him about Dr. X.
That to advance, you have to have your channels opened. It is
$500 plus $375 for two nights at the camp.

The healer smiles. "Your channels are already open."

The Chinese girl in my office, who had always been sup-
portive of my chi study, looks startled when I tell her I am
going to have my channels opened and asks me what kind of
chi gong I am studying.

"He charges five hundred dollars to open channels? He is
not the real thing. You have to look hard for a real master, in
the hills of China. They do not advertise. They do not charge
that."

I am beginning to feel that this mysterious channel opening might be . . . well . . . but I made arrangements to go to
the chi retreat. I remind them I can't sleep in a dorm. Too
much snoring.

I get special treatment. The woman who is arranging my
private room says she had a family emergency and couldn't
make it to the chi retreat the weekend she was supposed to

have her channels opened so Master X opened them from a few hundred miles away.

"What did you feel? What happened?"

"I don't really know," she confides. "But I'm sure something did."

I tell the Chinese girl Dr. X can open channels from 200 miles away.

"Does he think he is God?" she asks. I tell her more. She shakes her head. "Sounds like brainwashing." Yeah. I had to admit it sounded far-fetched.

I am in my private room. I am doing it despite my burgeoning skepticism. I am here to receive Zhong Gong—to have my "channels opened" by Master X.

A flyswatter in puce—make that "Barney" purple—is the only decoration in my room here at my first chi weekend at Camp Pontiac located in Copake, New York, in the foothills of the Berkshire Mountains.

I am alone in a trailer, tilted as if sinking into quagmire. The door does not shut all the way. Half the bolt has been removed. The walls are made of bits of compressed wood to form a sort of scrap-wood paneling. As if scraps of wood were run over by a steamroller. There is a strip of windows. One is boarded up.

And when I remove the dusty, wavy-foam padding on the mattress, I find, neatly in the center, like a chocolate left by the turn-down service, a giant water bug, feet up. And I had the luxury suite. The other students slept in bunk beds or rather, on human-sized trays of wood upon which a sleeping bag could be placed.

I deposit my stuff and go to the main building. We sign in and are handed a folded piece of paper. Printed on mine is the number 5. Sally gets the same number. A hand-made sign instructs us to buy the herbs that correspond to this number. "But it's random," I say. "It's another way to get money," she quips. "And maybe it's overstock. Or expired." We see Tania faithfully waiting to buy herbs.

Sally and I have been asking people for weeks, *What exactly is channel opening?* "It's very mysterious," comes the reply along with "it's beyond words," "it's different for everyone," and "it's an energetic connection," and "you'll have to see for yourself."

A student teacher tells us that after receiving Zhong Gong you cannot have sex for three months. They can't explain this. No one asks Dr. X why.

Next we choose linens. All the pillows are perfumed with mildew and mold except for one, which smells like an old man. Sally agrees it is the best.

On our way to hold the ball or "practice" in a smaller room, wiccas and warlocks, also staying at the camp, spread Tarot cards and grin in Goth/Renaissance-fair outfits. A man with black nail polish and lipstick reads palms. There is a table of items, possibly a raffle: a pinhead from *Hellraiser*, a ceramic wizard figurine holding a crystal ball in a box, three "magic" wands, tall candles in assorted colors, several books including one on fairies, a voodoo doll and a giant black lace bra. (Later my friend Craig Nelson will say, "It was worth five-hundred dollars just to see that!") But who are the real weirdos, here? Wait until they hear us "holding the ball."

Have I neglected to mention that it is off-season? Summer camp is long over. There is no heat. Anywhere.

What was I doing here with stinky pillowcases? Why am I wearing long silk underwear and LL Bean gear indoors? Why will I be sleeping on a water bug mattress?

We hold the ball while listening to moos, oms, wildcat cries, haunted house sounds, Three Stooges yelps, screams, stomping, rapid breathing, claps and more stomps. Dinner is Jiffy peanut butter, white bread . . . Remember—when your energy is aligned, you can eat anything. I've brought my own food.

Breakfast.

After seven A.M. practice (Seven A.M.?) This is still not working for me.

Zhuan Gong at nine-thirty. A guy I meet at breakfast says he ran for an hour with his eyes closed after the channel opening.

He explains that miraculously, after a channel opening, no one runs into any trees or bumps into anything.

There will be no running for any of us. Channel opening traditionally takes place outside and it is between Master X and the students with a few student teachers around. But it's pouring rain so we will do it indoors. In the room adjoining ours, the advanced students practice with full view of us, only a few wooden beams separating us. I feel like an animal on display, only they will be the ones making the animal sounds, not us.

The lights are out, and the dim rain-soaked atmosphere filters into the windows. Dr. X tells me to take off my shoes. I feel vulnerable. I don't see what possible harm there can be in keeping on my shoes. He explains I might slip in them due to the rubber sole. Slip? Why would channel opening make me slip? Am I going to do something erratic or crazy and leap and skip and whoop it up?

Someone tells me to remove all jewelry to eliminate magnetic resonance. Please, I said to myself, to the universe, to God—please let the channel opening feel like the heavens parting. Let it be beautiful. Let it be painful. I don't care. But please let me feel something, anything. Let it be real.

Dr. X walks behind us, five of us, our eyes are closed. Tania, Sally, me and two New Jersey students. This is the moment of truth. I don't feel anything. Nothing happens. I keep waiting. I wonder when it's going to happen. Then I am pushed in the shoulder and commanded to walk. I don't want to, I say. I am pushed harder. I wonder if the channel opening has to take effect this way, if I am supposed to have faith. I walk into a wall. I bump into a wooden beam. I hear other students making contact with hard surfaces. I can feel a breeze coming from the open door. With my eyes closed I head for it. I need to get out of here. I feel the edges of the door. I step over the threshold. I inhale the ozone and feel rain, I'm free, I'm free, but I am shoved back inside. This goes on for about an hour. The advanced students, whose channels are already opened, "practice" nearby and I remember reading a book about how water is affected by sounds and how ugly sounds deformed the water crystals and how beautiful things made them symmetrical and beautiful and I wonder if these anguished cries are affecting my immune system, making psychic dents in the structure of my sensitive cells.

Sitting in a circle, everyone who received Zhuan Gong discusses the experience. Tania says she felt something instantly, an energy, felt it was a gift.

Sally, who confides to me that she felt nothing, tells the group she welcomes the changes to come from having her channels opened.

I felt nothing but the residue of the psychic and physical abuse, the resentment and challenge of being forced to keep my eyes closed and to move around the room (Was I forced? Why did I consent?) on display for the advanced students. It brings back memories of dodge ball, of any sort of sport where I was forced to be a "team player," to endure physical aggression for the spectators. The whole thing was like "hazing."

"What exactly happens when channels are opened?" Tania asks.

"It's like having your satellite dish tuned into all the channels in the universe," says Dr. X. "Just the local channels are what you used to receive."

An advanced student asks, "If our master asks us to jump out the window, should we do it?"

"I never give a direct answer because I don't want to absorb your karma," says Dr. X.

"Is this how you practiced in China? I ask. "With animal noises and mental hospital screams?"

He crosses his arms like Yul Brynner in a bad mood in *The King and I.* "I make up my own, mixing soy sauce with ketchup."

"That ketchup is shorthand for capitalism," Sally whispers.

Later, a few people come up to me to tell me they've always been afraid to say what I did. One man says he questions the authenticity of people "sounding like their lungs are being ripped out." Someone else confides the screams used to bother her in the beginning but now it's "like fuzz."

I get a ride home from my sponsors.

I get into the apartment.

My husband greets me. "I have some kind of bad news. Something happened. Something broke. The tall Chinese vase in the bedroom. It just broke. It shattered. Spontaneously."

I tell my father, Leon, a professor and scholar of Sinology, whose newest book is *Imperial China, The State Cult of Confucius.* He laughs. "That vase got bad vibes from *somebody!*"

I didn't mind losing the vase. What's a vase? In the past year I'd paid over $10,000 to Dr. X.

I simply "let it go." I had to admit that this powerful practice had kept me healthy. Master X has charisma with more than a pinch of Svengali-ism. Whether it was placebo, or the power of chi, I was saved . . . but the "proof"—my vase—was shattered.

But out of some strange curiosity, a desire to complete the journey, I attended the advanced class. Dr. X did not teach it. I didn't feel compelled to clean the floor or polish plant leaves. We sat in a circle and talked and everyone asked about the "chi babies," those of us who'd just had our "channels opened." I asked a question and was reprimanded by another student. A young man defended my question saying I was not questioning the practice, they'd misunderstood. (They had not misunderstood: I was questioning the practice, apparently forbidden.) Someone else criticized me for not cleaning. Afterward, we "practiced." The students made wild sounds, slashed the air with their arms and squirmed on the floor. I never went back. I had my own apartment to clean.

Touch Me

It's bitingly cold, yet here I am, naked under a nubby cotton sheet in Mexico about to get my first healing massage. A house call, no less. I'm treating myself. Every year I make it through the holidays and past New Year's, a time dark with memories, it's cause for celebration. Joy, my host, said that BJ is rare, a natural-born healer, that he comes and goes from San Miguel de Allende and does not live in one place. Grab the chance.

BJ is a big man with gorgeous Led Zeppelin hair and beautifully large hands. No wonder he's in demand. Dressed simply in baggy orange pants and a plain white T-shirt worn soft as if it's been washed a thousand times, he exudes a Buddha-like calm. This calmness is as big as his body. I'm about to shake his hand, but he fixes a steady gaze on me, and I forget what I was about to do.

Upstairs, in the guest bedroom where I'm staying, BJ moves around the portable massage table where I lie. The lights flick on, then off. The power's unpredictable here. So's the hot water. I've been chilled ever since I arrived in San Miguel a couple of weeks ago. My favorite thing to do on Christmas is to be in the air, losing the actual day in time zones and transit so by the time I arrive at my destination, it's over. Then I'm in another country for New Year's, the most difficult time of all.

My breathing sounds unnaturally loud to me, and ragged. I must be anxious. I stare at a 3-D picture of the Virgin taped to the wall. This one's got dolorous brown eyes and a hot red mantilla. A few inches away, a bleached animal skull stares at me with empty eye sockets. Virgins and Death. So Mexico.

Six P.M. Dusk. The hundred bells of San Miguel chime, peal, clang, ring, toll through the thin mountain air in mad randomness. When BJ touches me, my skin vibrates along with the crazy bells. What is it about a stranger's touch? The hourly cacophony sets off the birds, with whom I share Joy's guest room. One cage holds two parakeets. The other cage holds three shy baby red-crowned Amazons. They chirrup and whistle and flap their tiny wings around the cages.

In between rescuing dogs and mentoring orphans, Joy bought and saved these birds from street sellers. Once they are grown, she will release them back into the wild. She is that kind of woman. I am not, though I'm not sure what kind of woman I am. Sometimes being motherless has that effect. You lack the blueprint. I think about the word *desmadres*, which literally means "without mother" but also means "mess."

BJ takes my feet in his hands. A vague panic stirs. "This is going to hurt," he says softly. "I want you to breathe through the pain." Even his voice radiates peace. Still, I feel my body stiffen. This doesn't feel like massage-as-pampering. Does he know the town's Inquisitioner used to live four doors down? That a conquistador used to live here? Does he sense that this house, with its gracious twenty-foot ceilings and six-foot-thick walls, is known to hold ghosts? A cold draft blows over me, and I shiver.

Just as I'm about to talk, tell him about the former bull-fighter-turned-love-balladeer with the rainbow-painted motorcycle helmet I met in the square earlier, or ramble about the ancient art of massage, or ask what it's like to be an ex-pat—my conversational gambits are as numerous as the town's bells—BJ wisely anticipates:

"It's best if you don't talk." This guy has my number.

He kneads my feet, and it feels prayerful, even when he rocks his bony fists in the flat arches.

Then he moves his big hands onto my lower legs. And stays there. Goes deeper. Then deeper still. His hands now are shovels, picks, prying and parting dense muscle. Minutes later it feels like daggers spring from my shins, fire sprouts from my calves. Still he won't let up on my lower legs. I lose track of time. The pain flares, plunges. It's a matter of pride that I don't cry out. I couldn't talk if I wanted to. It's taking every ounce of concentration just to avoid saying, *Stop. I can't stand it.*

Pain makes me hyper-aware. Every cell's at attention. The

birds chirr, their tiny scaled feet scraping over birdseed and clanging quietly against cage wire. The rescue dogs bark. I hear meat bones flung on the cold tile floor down in the kitchen. The hollow thud, the scrabble of dog nails, and even the slobber of their doggy mouths. The pain is sharpening my hearing. I can suck the cold in through my mouth, though my legs are aflame.

Under BJ's pressing, I feel my right thigh ripple under my kilt as I charge once again down the grass field in Cranford, New Jersey. I played center half, which meant I had license to chase you and smash your shins with my hockey stick to get the ball. I was living there because my mother lost custody. She couldn't take care of me anymore, so from age eleven I bounced from one home to another. I carried my aggression with me. In Alabama, where I moved with a foster family, I was captain of the school volleyball team, and a fearsome player on St. Andrew's Episcopal Church team, the Holy Terrors. Never mind I didn't then believe in God. I spiked the volleyball into people's faces till they cried for Jesus. No mercy. In college, I tackled a girl on the rugby field and sent her to the hospital with a split-open jaw. I can taste the old physical fury like a mouthful of habanero.

I squeeze my eyes shut. BJ inexorably works his way up to my thighs, where the hurt intensifies. Pinwheels of pain spin out from thickly braided muscles. Spark and lift off. I white-knuckle the sides of the massage table. "Your right leg," BJ says, "is strong." He prods a thumb gently but determinedly into a bunched muscle. "Too much energy here. That can block flow. You need more *internal* strength."

Maybe. I've heard this before, from yoga instructors. They too saw what I hid beneath my external strength; they saw my core was weak in comparison. More vulnerable. For years I built showy muscles, fed a violent drive.

"Let's turn you over," says BJ. I turn over. The sheet is wet with sweat. BJ drops a scratchy wool blanket on top, seeing my goose bumps. My legs are pulsing. Then it feels like BJ thrusts his hand directly into the center of my quad, hitting a hidden clump of electric tension. It's like he's unleashed grade VI whitewater rapids in there.

"Relax," BJ says. "Breathe." I do. My legs are churning, thrumming, stifling in their sheeted cocoon when all I want to do is run.

BJ plants his big hands on my back, and instantly a new wave of pain begins. My proud back, with the ridge in the middle from years of crew and weight lifting. Knots of muscles lattice the ribs. Bowlines, monkey's fists, slipknots. I feel one of these knots unravel.

Joy has guilted me into joining her on the annual orphan girl outing to the Tuesday Mercado. At the end of the long day, I see myself kneeling in the chalky dust of the Mercado parking lot, tying one orphan girl's shoelaces on her beat-up boots. Earlier this orphan girl stuck her tongue out at me. She is stubborn, already hard-faced at eight years of age. The laces on her boots are dusty, cracked. The plastic tips are long gone, so it's hard to thread the ends; I find myself spitting into my hand to create a point for the bootlace. The boot is creased like a centurion's face. *My mother is on vacation*, the orphan girl says, clutching her plastic bags of cheap sweaters and sunglasses and *zapatos* to her side, looking directly at me with hooded eyes, like she's telling me a secret. *She's coming back.* And she grips her plastic bags tightly.

My brain shorts out as BJ presses on a knot. I am suddenly famished. Since arriving in Mexico, I have eaten green chorizo and gotten acute turista. I have eaten *nopales*, cactus. Picked up candy from a piñata busted at the stroke of midnight by a group of manic kids and eaten that too. My hunger is inexhaustible. Now, as BJ digs into my shoulder blades, a sugary liqueur of sadness suffuses every vein, pumping sluggishly. That weight I bore on my shoulders, it falls, tumbles, and bumps—rolls away into a corner like a sullen globe of the world.

I open my eyes for a moment. Pretty paper lanterns swing weirdly in the draft from an open window. Someone nearby puts on a record. Pedro Vargas. The sound is unbearably melancholic, warm and soulful. They say the bells of San Miguel were sweetened by gold, when the bell maker melted down his dead lover's jewelry.

I am floating on the singer's notes. The almond-scented oil has simmered into my skin. I'm thinking we're done, I made it, I'm still a tough girl. Then BJ places his hands around my neck.

When I was in college, a woman with green tilted eyes and velveteen lashes gave me a gift certificate for a massage. This seemed an incredibly luxurious gift. How it happened, we were in her room smoking clove cigarettes, talking about Gertrude Stein, and then, on impulse, I told her about my mother. When she gathered me in her arms that night, and held me on that narrow dorm bed, and kissed my hair and neck, I fell in love. Love was more fluid then. Never mind we barely did anything. When she touched my thigh, I burned. I drove her to Cape Cod for a weekend to stay at Mrs. Fay's beachside guest cottage, thinking bravely, stupidly, this would be our time. Once during that weekend, when I was sitting on her lap and kissing her, she pushed me away. *What would Mrs. Fay say if she walked in now? Gee, er, Mrs. Fay, I really like my friend!* She was gay, and did not want to be. I was not. I was just in love, and free, then. I didn't care. You see, she reminded me of my mother. So when this woman picked up a coil of boat rope and wrapped it around her neck, and knotted it, and began tightening it, turning her neck red, saying, *I should just strangle myself*—her green eyes stubborn and glittering with what I realize in retrospect was intense homophobic panic—I freaked. I pleaded. Then I held her knees and laid my head by her feet, for a very long time. Until she let the rope drop away.

After Cape Cod, this woman disappeared from my life. I never did use that gift certificate. I kept delaying, thinking: *I'm not tired enough. I haven't worked hard enough. I haven't earned a massage yet. Maybe after finals. Maybe after crew season. Maybe in springtime.* Until it expired.

I allow myself massages only when I'm traveling. In Shanghai, in a smoke-filled room lit only by an aquarium and the glow of cigarettes, I was massaged by a blind man with fingers like sea anemones; in Thailand, at the Temple of the Reclining Buddha, in a room decorated with gold, jam-packed with cots, a Thai man padded on my back, turning it into a bridge of flesh and conjuring ancient childhood trauma; in Tahiti, lush-hipped women rolled and stroked my skin with touches soft as the petals of a *tiare*.

I know that massage has the power to pull memory from muscle.

But even with my body a gridwork of pain, I was not prepared for what BJ did next in that freezing cold guest room in San Miguel.

BJ lightly touches my neck, and for the first time that day—I flinch. I wasn't expecting tenderness. I realize I've been braced for pain; that's easier. He pauses. I listen to him sigh softly. This is also the first time he's sighed. What is going on? My heart pounds. I feel his breath on my neck as he moves in closer. Then BJ digs his thumbs deep into my neck, and holds them there for a long time. Tears spring from the corners of my eyes, spill onto the cold tile floor. Slowly, he moves his fingers around, and down, digging, deep, circling the whole throat. Finally his fingers splay and grasp, cradle and probe, all at once, as if tugging me by the very root of my skull, here into the fresh new world. Reborn. BJ says nothing, keeps working on my neck, though he sighs wearily. I don't know why, but this breaks my heart. Soon I am weeping. Gutbucket, wracking sobs. In a way you never do in front of anyone. Let alone a stranger.

Or only a stranger. With anyone else, the stakes are too high. There is too much to lose with such exposure. Only a stranger. Or God.

For this is how my mother died: hanging herself by a rope

tied around a beam in the attic of her parents' house in Do-
ver, Massachusetts, on New Year's Eve, 1977. This year it will
be thirty years since her death. Sometimes that feels like an
eternity. Sometimes it feels like today.

Dr. Shannon O'Kelly

Dr. Shannon O'Kelly is a New York–based practitioner of "Net-work," a form of chiropractic that involves no cracking. The other big difference is that she treats four people at once, laid out next to one another on tables.

The raw emotions are released differently with each person you encounter. Like when someone starts bursting into laughter on the table, during or after. Or even sobbing. If you think about it, crying and laughing are the same emotion. Just different spectrums. It's just a different form of release. My job is not to let that interfere with healing. In my personal experience no one has done anything on the table inappropriate or crossed any lines to make me feel uncomfortable; of course I've heard about it, but I don't think in a group room, especially, it would go down.

At the beginning of my practice, my first thought was that I wasn't going to be friends with my clients and patients. I wanted to keep it separate. Then, after a few years, I realized these are the people that get it. These are the people who are tuned in, and want to connect with their higher self. And those are the people I want to keep company with. And at some point, my theory switched. Of course, certain ones I connect with more than others. For instance, one of my practice members took me to the U.S. Open last night, and it was awesome. She knew I loved tennis, and we sat front row.

There's always friends that fall out of coming here, and I still love them. It just depends. You always have to have boundaries, with any relationship. But it's a good pool of people to have as your spiritual family. Of my close friends, for instance, my acupuncturist and I are very close. We met while working in the same office. We were both traveling to Thailand, both speak Thai. Both being practitioners, we had a common understanding. I trusted her to use needles on me, which I was really afraid of at first.

The office is a certain setting. Professional setting, and even when the most intimate things do happen, because they will, they don't happen here. A pelvis opening, for instance. The patient would then go home, and have sex. Hopefully. The personal acts we help people to reach do not happen in the office. But in the clients' private lives.

With success, and clientele, and freedom of choosing how much you're charging, you don't have to put up with, say, a client's phone call at midnight asking for an adjustment.

Of course there's exceptions. I would do so for my close friends, but not all my patients can be my friends. That goes along with the trust, and knowing, with the select few, you can't help it. There's just that connection.

Body Lessons

LENA LEVIN

For years, my father gave my mother the most luxurious birthday present he could imagine: a gift certificate for a massage. My mother would open the thin red box with appropriate rapture. Then, strangely, months would go by. Eventually she'd submit her slender, pale shoulders to the hands of the masseuse. At least, that's what I assumed.

I was in my thirties the year she called me up and said, "Take the certificate, honey. You'll enjoy it more than I will."

"But it's your birthday present," I said. "I can't."

"Why not?" my mother said. "I've never liked massages. I wish you'd take it and get some pleasure from it."

I was amazed. Why had she pretended to enjoy all those gifts? And how could my mother have a problem with touch? After all, she embraced me every time we met—long, tender hugs, so that I knew the texture of her cheek, the delicate narrows of her back. But then I began to think about who, exactly, besides me and my father, was permitted contact with my mother's body.

She did her own manicures—I thought she liked unpainted nails. She colored her own hair—I thought she'd found her perfect auburn. She gave herself haircuts—I thought she figured no one could tell, the way she coiled her hair up with combs.

"Oh, I'll get pleasure from it," I said. "But why don't you?"

It would take nearly a decade for my mother's answer to finish falling, like a stone, through the polished lake into which I sink my old, unspeakable memories.

"I don't like being handled by strangers," my mother said.

When I was thirteen or so, my best friendships involved the scratching of backs—ten minutes of yours, ten minutes of mine. It was shivery bliss. A few years later, when blackheads peppered our backs, the ritual expanded: You squeeze mine, I'll squeeze yours. We might as well have been high in the trees, safe from predators, picking nits from each other's fur.

After squeezing, of course, we scratched. It was innocent, exquisite. Touch without threat. It was better than what boys wanted. What else was skin for?

Skin, a boundary as fragile as antique silk, is there to be transgressed. This is going to happen. And when it starts, it must be endured until it stops.

This lesson was transmitted though my family's marrow. I can track it back three generations to a tiny town in Russia called Cominets Podalsk, until I lose all trace of our name.

How the body learns: My grandmother Perle was nine when she had to quit school. Food was scarce, and her parents needed the extra income. On dark winter dawns, she walked alone past a graveyard, which terrified her, to a factory where she rolled cigarettes. Perle kept her coat on all day, for warmth, and pocketed her gloves, for dexterity. When tobacco sifted through her icy fingers to the floor, the boss's wife shot over, enraged. "Your blood should spill as you spill mine," she shouted at the child.

Later, she would educate herself from books. But the education of her body was early, and swift: Transgressions must be endured. She spent her childhood in fear of pogroms— the murderous rampages of Gentiles against Jews—and in dread of her father, who drank, and came after her with his fists.

Families emigrated one person at a time back then. Perle's father kept up the beatings till she boarded a ship for New York. She was thirteen, possessed of a stunning bosom, entrusted to the care of an adult who was making the weeks-long journey too—a family friend, a man.

I accepted my mother's birthday massage. After all, I loved being handled by strangers. Didn't I? Why else would I go back again and again for certain small, sensory delights: having my hair reddened, my muscle knots released, my nails brushed with delirious hues of blue?

Handled: an uncomfortable, hard-fingered word. It snagged at my subconscious, a fish hook in the polished lake.

During my weekly mani-pedi, the pedicurist, massaging

my right foot, pushes on the pea-sized sesamoid bone. I gasp. Ten years ago, I broke the sesamoid landing a hard jump on Rollerblades. Now it feels like she's jabbing a needle into the ball of my foot.

The pedicurist looks up, wondering what hurt.

"Oh, it's fine," I say, biting my lip. Reassured, she does it again. The sesamoid flares. I pray it won't crack along its calci-fied, arthritic seam.

I cannot speak.

How the body learns: I coax my mother to the hair salon, because she's admired my haircut, and I like my stylist. Bad idea. The stylist cuts her hair too short. Then she teases it too high, so my mother's scalp shows rabbity and pink, and puffs up the bangs, normally silky and long. My mother is an elegant woman. She has cheekbones tipped at an exotic angle and a fondness for good scarves, fully-lined slacks, black pumps. Now she has cute hair.

It's my stylist, so maybe I should pipe up: "That doesn't look right. Let's get it wet and do the blow-dry again." But perhaps that's my mother's job. Isn't it? She's the client now. It's her hair.

I look at her questioningly. *What do you want to do?* She looks back brightly. *Let's just get out of here, shall we?* She can't speak up either, I realize. We're both stuck. Sadness settles through me. We smile at the stylist.

"Very nice," says my mother, slowly. "Artful. Thank you."

My mother drives, her delicate hands resting on the wheel. We're affectionate with each other, but gingerly too. We agree that one has to get used to a new cut. We trade blow-drying tips. We act like two women who can say what they please. We pretend she is not going home to wash the hands of a stranger out of her hair.

How the body learns: My mother is a teenager in upstate New York, listening, rapt, at a girlfriend's house as the friend describes arguing with her own mother.

"And then what?" my mother asks, leaning forward, because the story just trails off.

"Then nothing," says her friend, confused. "We made up."

My mother too is confused. Made up how? In her own house, when Perle gets angry, there is only this: Flee to the bathroom. Lock the door. Spend minutes, hours, sitting on the hard tile floor, arms wrapped around her knees. It makes no difference. When my mother emerges, Perle is waiting—broad of shoulder, implacable with rage. In her hand is a wooden hanger.

Skin is made to be transgressed.

My mother tells me about Perle when I am fifteen. She says that Perle almost certainly got molested on that ship. Not that Perle said it outright, but it's something my mother believes.

"Who could have helped her?" my mother says, compassionately. "Who could she have told?"

A few years ago, I was massaged by a young woman who made no conversation. I liked the way she honored the privacy of the sheet, lifting one neat, careful corner at a time. Her silence fell over us both like a veil.

Well into the treatment, however, she broke into the peace of the candle-scented room.

"There's a form of massage that is specific to the breasts," she said. "Do you want me to do that?"

Did I want her to massage my *breasts*?

There is, let's be clear, a legitimate form of breast massage. It begins with the asking of consent. I had learned this at a physical therapy clinic, where a young masseuse named Lori labored over my knotted back. A male colleague, she told me, once worked on her breasts in a practice session. They were both in massage school. They were friends. He didn't ask.

"What did you do?" I thought she might reveal something I needed to hear—but I was disappointed.

"Absolutely nothing," said Lori. "I couldn't speak. I kept telling myself, 'It's OK, he's not being sexual,' and 'It's OK, we're friends.'" It wasn't OK. Three days later, she felt violated, enraged. She called her friend and said, "I never want to speak to you again."

My masseuse, her hand on the sheet, stood waiting. Did I want my breasts massaged?

My skin too has been transgressed. Not by an act of violence: My mother, an extraordinary woman, broke with the family legacy and never struck me. I was *interfered with* by someone I worked for as a teenager.

Molest: I looked it up. It means to bother. To annoy. To persecute with hostile intent. To subject to unwanted sexual activity. To force sexual contact on, as with a child. To disturb. To interfere with.

You might say I was too old to call it molestation.

You might say it was just sexual harassment.

You might say it went on too long.

You might say I should have quit.

You might say I was to blame, a grown girl of seventeen, but I've already said it.

You might say I had worked it out in therapy since then.

You might say that two decades later the waters of the lake were still.

You might say I had learned to be easy in my body, not like my mother, not a woman saying no to lavish forms of touch.

You might say if I consented to the breast massage, I'd be in full control.

You might say that I was forty years old, and knew damn well how to say stop.

The candles smelled of jasmine. From a courtyard came the rippling sound of running water. The sheet lay cool on my stomach.

So. Did I want my breasts massaged?

I did not think: *What happens when a person who has been transgressed lies down on a massage table, unzips body boundaries as porous as lace, and hands control to a total stranger?*

I did not think: *Flashback*. I did not think: *Paralysis*.

I did not think about my mother, who I pray ripped up those gift certificates year after year.

I did not think. I was too busy admiring the surface of the lake, obsidian-hard and sleek.

"Sure," I said. "Go ahead."

Moving like a nurse, the masseuse folded down the sheet and went to work.

It was not erotic, as I'd thought it might be. Nor was it

relaxing. I'm thin, with small breasts, subject to bouts of body loathing, and as she aligned her fingers with my ribs, I thought, *Stop looking at my fucking chest.* Angry? Why was I angry? Her touch was one of detached expertise, yet I began to panic. How does one call off the handling of one's body by a stranger? I already knew the answer to that, passed down, without words, from my great-grandfather to my grandmother to my mother to me: You don't. An act of violation will continue until it stops.

The longer I stayed mute, the more I hated the breast massage. And the more I hated the breast massage, the more I fantasized about sitting up and socking the massage therapist in the face.

When it was over, I dressed, paid, left a nice tip, and slid into the car. Why was I trembling? She had asked. I didn't say no. *But you wanted to*, I thought. Something seemed to swell inside my throat, as if my vocal cords had been stitched down hard for years, and I had a sudden desire to scream.

How the body learns: When my mother was eleven, a family friend—a man—took her on a long bus journey. My grandmother, strangely, arranged this. During the trip, the man draped his arm around my mother's shoulder. She did not know what to say. He slid his hand down her blouse. She did not know what to say. He gripped her breast, which had barely begun to develop. He kept his grip on her there for the rest of the way.

She did not know how to speak at all.

She told me this.

She also told me other things, designed to keep me safe

as a child: Run from strangers who want directions, who offer candy, who say they've lost a kitten in the park. In turn,
when my son was about four, I began passing these lessons
on. Don't be polite, I told him. If someone touches you in a
bad way, be rude. Be loud. I don't care if it's a teacher or a
doctor or the lady next door. Say no in a big voice. And I will
always, always back you up.

I even made him yell it: *Don't touch me like that!*

My son sat cross-legged on his bed, surrounded by bits of
red and yellow LEGO, and bellowed happily, "Don't touch
me like that!"

But this is how the body learns: A mother sits on the subway with her little boy. She has not yet had her breasts massaged. And she has never told a soul, not even her husband or
her therapist, exactly what she did for her boss. (Exactly what
he made you do, her therapist would correct.) She will die
before she tells. In this lesson her son is about six, dressed in
private-school polo and khakis. The subway's rocketing along,
it's a crowded hour, and a man squeezes in beside the little
boy.

The man starts talking to himself.

Immobilized, the mother tunes in—glances over, just barely, from the white of her eye. The man is nudging her son,
mumbling to him and prodding him with an elbow. The boy
stares straight ahead with Power Ranger intensity. The mother prickles into a sweat. The man mutters and nudges. Across
the subway car, people watch leadenly from their orange plastic seats, shifting their gazes from the mother to the child to
the mumbling man. What can she do? If she leads her child

away, will the man grow angry, even dangerous? You cannot tell with strangers.

But that is not the reason she's frozen, and she knows it. She is just . . . stuck. She is Perle on the ship. She is her own mother on that bus. They're getting off at the next stop anyway. The man keeps muttering, and nudging, and the train grumbles into the next gray station.

You might think that when they get off, the mother finds a way to make it better. Maybe she says, "Whew, I'm glad we got away from that creep. What a creep, huh?"

Instead, this mother pretends she did not have all the facts.

She asks her son, gently, what the man was saying. Just crazy stuff, her son says. But he kept pushing me too.

Pushing you? The mother acts appalled. Like shoving you? Like bumping? Baby, I'm so sorry. If I had known, we could have moved. I thought he was just some guy talking to himself, and I knew we'd be getting off the train.

But she had known. And her son is aware that she knew. She can feel this.

The platform's narrow and dangerous. He won't move till she takes his hand. His fingers are small and damp in hers. Papers flutter on the tracks. She is a rotten mother, teaching rotten lessons. Transgression must be endured. The lake is swirling with silt now, and she is frantic to make it stop.

Listen to me, she says. If someone touches you in a bad way, you have to speak up. Are you listening, honey? It's your job to say, Mommy, this man is bothering me. Mommy can't help you if you don't speak up.

Of course it was not the massage therapist I hated. It was myself, for not saying no.

I was not even entirely present when she rubbed my breasts.

I was back in a brightly lit store, thirty years earlier, staring at the shag carpet because I could not look at my boss, could not parse the words for *Are you out of your fucking mind?*

"My back," he would say, and sag against the wall. Smoke curled up from his fingers; he was never without a lit cigarette. "The shrapnel, it is killing me. I cannot stand the pain." He'd been a hero in the Six Day War, though he was slope-shouldered now, and sallow. I was nothing, a salesgirl, untrusting, shaming him with my lack of trust. When I hesitated, his face would flicker with annoyance.

"Come upstairs," he would say, locking the glass door of the store and turning the sign around: "Closed." It was always the same, the display cases glaring halogen-white, our footfalls sucked into the silent carpet.

"Don't be afraid," he would say, one hand pressed to the small of his back. "I just need you to give me a massage."

The Stripper's Best Friend

Anonymous

It had not crossed my mind that strip clubs employ in-house makeup artists, until I was pointed in the direction of "Lady X," who must remain anonymous for fear of being fired. I will tell you she lives in a major U.S city, works for a major club, and is majorly smart.

I was turning forty. And I had an agent, and I was freelancing on films and TV. I liked working fifteen hours at a time, for six weeks at a time. Then I'd be done. But then you find yourself unemployed. And after a while, there was just always a feeling of loss, and a depression afterward. I would go through a withdrawal from humanity. From going from being so close to somebody, then professionally . . . it just ends.

What's great about this job is the fact that I have a real relationship with this woman. I help her become who she wants to be. There's an emotional connection. To help her switch from college student to . . . you know. A lot of them are students. A lot of them are on visas. A lot of them are sending money to their families. I help turn such a hardworking person into a dancer. It's a transformation.

I work for three nights a week, and every other Sunday, and have three nights to myself. The money is good. There's a price for every service. Eyelashes are $10. It's the flat rate for covering tattoos, because not all clubs recommend them. Just applying eye makeup is $10. And then there's a minimum tip they give me a night. If there are thirty-four women dancing, I probably worked on seventeen of them.

The common things, everyone needs help with. Everything from making them look less tired. Maybe they had a rough day at work, or spent all day with their kids, and look exhausted. I cover bruising, everywhere from elbows to anywhere dancing affects. Most of them are doing aerobics all night. There are women that love it, and call themselves dancers. And there are women that do it, then go home to their lives. There's a huge separation, I always tell them when they're sitting in the chair, "This is just what you do, and not who you are. This is just what you do, so you can be who are." I like them to make that separation.

Most of them are young, they're in their twenties. The oldest dancer here is forty-four, and the youngest is nineteen. The older women don't usually dance as much as the younger ones. Men enjoy them and their company for different reasons, like good conversation. They can discuss politics. Put them in a private room, and they can talk for hours. And they enjoy their time spent with a bright woman.

The industry has changed so much. It used to look like Barbie dolls. And they all had perky breasts. Now there's a culture change. It goes along with a change in society. We have women here that are very flat, like boys. We have women that are more full-figured than you think. Very round, tall, very short. Every nationality and color and race. Men like different things. Some men ask specifically for woman without breast implants. And others ask for the huge cartoon boobs.

To think of these women as weak, or completely insecure with themselves, is a misjudgment, to say the least. I used to think that they had more issues with liking themselves than the common corporate type. Then after being around it for years, I compared those feelings with women I have in my life, it's pretty much exactly the same.

These women make a living with their figures. The world is watching them; too many of them are really hard on themselves. When asking men if they would like a dance, and men respond no, then they go through the common emotions of thinking it must be them, their body, their something. They subconsciously ask themselves, Well what's wrong with me? And they do cry, in the dressing room. I do the makeup, and I stay in the dressing room. And if they are having a rough night, they assume it's their fault.

Usually at this time in the night, all the makeup's done, and I have a few hours left to read magazines. And one by one, after they dance, they'd come backstage to vent. Telling themselves they don't like me, I must have to get work done. But truly it doesn't matter if you're forty or twenty-four, no woman likes her nipples. I like seeing the many different shapes of women, and enjoy feeling like I'm just another piece of the wide range.

A lot of them are businesswomen, very smart. And I do their makeup. I have regulars. I fit the eyes with their outfit. They always trust me. That's extremely important.

I never open up my private life. I'm the listener. I like being their support system. With all the politics going on in here, under no circumstances can you be a gossip.

I was molested as a child, and a high proportion of these women were too, or had a bad experience somewhere along the line. It means so much to me that I am the last person they see before they go out there. I feel like I'm making a difference.

There's so much that goes on. The managers, they think I'm just a makeup artist.

And that I know nothing. Truth being, I actually know a lot more than anyone thinks.

PART IV

Unhand Me, Fiend

ANNIE LYNCH

Annie is originally from a very small town in Iowa called Clive. It's a very slow suburb of Des Moines. She left her hometown at the age of seventeen (she was a young graduate of her high school class) and moved to Southern California in hopes of becoming a movie star. She moved in with her grandparents, in Long Beach, California, and shortly thereafter began classes at Cal State Long Beach, studying modern dance and hip-hop, with a major in dietetics and kinesiology—physical therapy.

I really had high hopes and aspirations for taking dance extremely far. I know I don't seem like the typical hip-hopper, but with thirteen years of extensive dance, and Madonna being my all-time love, I truly believed I'd be shaking my rump in videos in no time. I still want to continue my dancing career, and will someday be in a video. But I got really into all the health classes I had to take as part of my dance program at Cal State. One of which was Pilates. I fell in love. I couldn't get enough: all the endorphins released. I was addicted to the feeling Pilates gave my body, and mental state. Any free time I had went to reading, research, and branching out to local Pilates studios, to seek this high, and just take in all the information I possibly could. I really have the exact same thoughts toward Pilates as I did the first time I took a class, and felt my body just literally say "ahhhhh." I wanted everyone to feel as good as I did! Then I took a super-advanced class at Cal State, and a certain wonderful teacher/instructor took me under her wing, and became my mentor. She believed in me, and my people/teaching skills, and friendly demeanor so much, she gave me a $1,000 scholarship, to get certified.

My teacher actually opened this studio about four years ago. And after I got certified, I was teaching for her. You'd be surprised at all the different types of people that are all hard-core Pilates. Ranging from bored-as-fuck housewives with huge rocks on their fingers, to sassy rockabilly tattooed chicks, to young high school athletes. It's obviously a more female-driven atmosphere, but I do deal with a lot of male clients. Whether they try it because their wife made them come, or the teens are so pressured to look so goddamn perfect in those tiny volleyball shorts . . . they end up seeing the change in their body.

I remember trying it for the first time, and the machinery alone looks completely terrifying. It reminded me of some intense, crazy, sex swing/bondage-looking torture straps. So many people are so nervous and apprehensive about strappin' in and slidin' around. So nervous to bend and pull their body, especially in front of me, touching them, guiding them. And

after all the pulling and tugging, the flexibility increases im-
mensely . . . so they can apply that in other areas.

*Annie had been living in Long Beach for five years and work-
ing at the studio for two. On October 19, 2006, following up
on a persistent cough, her doctor, to the amazement of Annie,
her clients and family, diagnosed her with lymphoma, cancer
of the lymph nodes. On November 5 the pathology results came
in: non-Hodgkins lymphoma, spreading fast. Annie's frightening
news was compounded by the fact that she is one of America's
forty-four million uninsured. With her mother sick herself and
her father not in the picture, Annie's older sister took her in with
her husband and children in Minnesota for the first round of
chemo. In sunny Long Beach, where most girls' biggest fear is
how they look in their bikini, and Annie was known as a local
beauty, she had been famous for her long, shiny black hair. In
snowy Minnesota, she took the plunge and shaved her head, then
put the photos up on MySpace.*

I need to put new pictures up, actually, 'cos this is the real
deal now. I have no hair on the left side of my head and my
eyebrows are about to fall out. One of my favorite dance teachers from L.A. was just here and I felt so comfortable I took
off my wig and just sat there. At first, I didn't think I would
want to wear a wig. I said I'd wear handkerchiefs. Then your
hair falls out and you feel people are looking at you. Sometimes you just want to fit in, go out to dinner, blend in rather
than being "cancergirl." The cancer society has a class I went
to called "Look good . . . feel better!" I was the only woman
under forty-five. The others have breast cancer. But we're all
dealing with no eyebrows and yellow skin. They teach you
how to do the makeup, give you a bag of it to take away.

Everyone on MySpace loved the shaved head. But I'll tell the truth: I definitely didn't let go of vanity overnight. My hair was so beautiful! it was really hard for me. But I knew that it would be easier in the end. I don't want all of the sudden people to see me twenty pounds lighter and yellow. That's why I posted those pictures. All of the sudden you're faced with something that's not in your hands and the only power you have over your diagnosis is the way you look at it.

In Long Beach, I didn't have a boyfriend but I'd go out and meet guys and get numbers and randomly make out with guys here and there. Normal twenty-three-year-old girl. I don't feel like the sexual being I was—the medicine I'm on takes the energy out of you—but I definitely still desire. Everyone desires to be desired. I don't know if that's the age of MySpace or human nature. And of course, I feel not as pretty to guys. And if they are attracted to you, when do you throw out the "I'm going through chemo so I can't hang out and party!"?

Tomorrow my special, nice wig arrives and I'm so excited. Because I was uninsured, the oncology department gave me a $200 gift certificate to Merle Norman. The woman who helped had alopecia, and she started picking out wigs for me. I said I wanted the same long, black, sexy hair that I had before. But she talked me into more of an auburn wig in a bob. Because of the chemo, I'll be getting paler and paler and she explained that I'll need a little color because the dark wig will make me look sicker. This wig is so cute. I'll be putting that photo up on MySpace, for sure.

After five years in Long Beach I can definitely confirm that the beach body image is overwhelming in southern California. But the gift of Pilates is spreading good body image. That's part of why I loved it.

And I know that my background in dance and Pilates gave me greater strength to get through this. When I first got to the Minnesota Children's Hospital, I was on a ventilator. Once I was off that they gave me tasks, like, to try and sit up for thirty minutes and I'd say "No, forty-five!" It's about finishing and doing more than people expect. We're trying to raise money for my medical bills and I plan to be dancing by the benefit on December 22. Even though I have chemo on the 20th.

All my friends say "It's so unfair, you're the one who did Pilates every day, who was the healthy one." But that's the way thunder strikes. It's part of my path.

Because of the cancer, I got closer to my dad, who I had a bitter, bitter relationship with my entire life. My parents had divorced a long time ago and he has a big alcohol problem. When I called to tell him I had lymphoma spreading fast, he was drunk. And it's been a wake-up call for him. Now I'm helping my dad with his disease.

My Pilates clients back in Long Beach have been so amazing. One of my clients sent me a package of Rolling Stones T-shirts because she knows I worship them. A lot of them have made the donations they could to my bills. All of them gave me beautiful gifts before I left. I love all my clients so much, I don't even care if they love me.

Today I heard I'll be getting medical assistance from the state of Minnesota back-dated to November 24. From now on they're paying. Woo-hoo! So I have about $100,000 in medical bills to pay off somehow, then I'm free!

Now I feel even feistier about dancing, because there are new things I'll be telling through my choreography. But, after I pay off the $100,000, what I really want to do is open my own studio, Jinjer Pilates. Jinjer to make you think of a palate cleanser. I need it. And I can't wait.

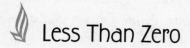 # Less Than Zero

BARBARA ELLEN

I wonder sometimes: When all those size zeros are on their deathbeds, will they push aside their nearest and dearest, shoo away their husbands dismissively, kick their children (if they have any) out of the room, and sink back onto their pillows, struggling for breath, just wanting to be left alone with their memories of when they were at their skinniest? Those halcyon days when the world was queuing up to tell them what every woman is always dying to hear, even when she's dying—You're too thin, you must put on weight, why, I can count your ribs through that beautiful (child-sized) gown, I can make out your internal organs jostling for position. The world is worried sick about you. Beside itself. It can talk of little else. You are just too thin. Now quick, before the mortician arrives, do you have any good diet tips?

Too thin doesn't impress me much. I was too thin for a

long time. It was no big achievement. It wasn't like I tried to be too thin, or studied for the privilege. I didn't wake up one morning with a mortarboard on my head, clutching a Ph.D. in "Advanced Scrawn." I was a natural. I didn't diet or exercise. I ate so many carbs I was probably more doughnut than woman. But still I was so skinny that complete strangers (the Food Disorder Police) would nudge each other in the street. So thin that friends—good friends, worried friends—would shoot each other covert looks when I clanked into bars to meet them, all skin, bone, hope, nerves, and cheap sticky lip gloss. But that was at a time when skinny wasn't the go-anywhere currency, the instant-esteem elixir, it is today.

Back then, it was the curvaceous girls who ruled the world. The girls ripe with breasts and rump (swollen with power). While I clattered through adolescence, trying to pretend my rib cage was a bust, it seemed as though all they had to do was stand there, with their womanly shape, and the boys would fly at them like hormonally charged staples to a magnet. That was how it worked then. No one ever gave my skinniness a standing ovation ("Girl, you are *working* that emaciation!"). No creepy, scrawn-worshipping website lauded me, and people like me, as "Thinspirations." Strange really, how my timing was so out of whack. I was born out of step with the body fashions of the times at both ends: born too soon to enjoy the twisted accolades of size zero, and yet, when I no longer had thighs like pencils, that became the sum of female desire.

Let's be clear though; don't romanticize the past— voluptuousness was one thing, plain old fat quite another. Looking back, you realize with a pang why all the plumper girls you've ever known tended to have immaculate glossy hair and shoe fetishes.

(These were the only things they could control.)

I push open the door of the gym.

My personal trainer is waiting. Personal trainers are what happen to people who commit the cardinal sin of no longer being too thin. Their role is to convince people not remotely interested in the sadomasochistic world that it is completely normal to pay someone to bully, criticize, and insult you. (All the things that, in a regular relationship, would kill passion as surely as a swatted fly.)

My personal trainer has baby Rasta dreads and the color of skin I would have liked (cappuccino, glowing, low maintenance). Because he is so attractive, he has lasted longer than the rest, but that does not necessarily mean he will last much longer. He has already begun stalking me by telephone to remind me about appointments (the fact that I told him to is irrelevant). He has already made it clear that I am horribly unfit (the fact that I told him to be "brutally honest" doesn't excuse the honesty or the brutality). Then there is that aura he has (they all have)—of physical superiority, silent criticism.

Sometimes not so silent.

At my initial weigh-in and health check, my BMI was 22, perfectly reasonable for my height, but not according to him. "It's the wrong kind of 22, an *untoned* 22." (Why do gym people always intone the word *untoned*?) Something like the old teen rebellion (in some of us, never dead, just sleeping) flared. Was he trying to sell me a body even the medical community agreed I didn't need? Do they make it up—all this crap? (Whisper it.) Do we want them to? How many of us are delivered into the heartless hell of body fascism by the feminine night trains of paranoia and low self-esteem?

Anyway it still rankles.

Innocent of my inner mutiny, the personal trainer takes me through some warm-up exercises. Bend my arm back. "Bring up the other hand and hold." Slide my hand along one hip and down. "Lower than that." Now touch my toes.

"I can't." (He knows I can't; I have hamstrings like truncated rubber bands.)

He says nothing, just walks away, leaving me crouched there, grappling feebly with my upper calves.

"The bike first," he says.

Obediently I start to pedal. It is all I can do not to scream.

For some of us the gym is a spaghetti of paradoxes. It is an arena dedicated to strength, but when I am in it, I feel at my absolute weakest. It is a temple to the Body Beautiful, but when I am there, I feel at my ugliest. It is a brick poem to health and vigor, but for me the flattest, most lifeless prose I've ever seen. It is supposed to be your best shot at eternal youth, but one hour spent toiling within these walls and I am a hundred years older than when I first walked in.

I know, I have always known, that this is not my world.

Silently, arms folded, he watches me pedal. The air is full of judgment about my performance but I don't know why. (Too slow, too fast, should I be tipping back in my seat, shouting, "Geronimo!"?) We are surrounded by the standard equipment of the exercise torture chamber. Bikes, rowing machines, pulleys, treadmills. The balls upon which you roll and lurch around like an upturned turtle. Then there are the sensory hits. Sweat, red faces, macho grimacing from males and females alike. Crunchy socks jammed into damp plimsolls. Water bottles drained and refilled at communal fountains that somehow taste of swimming pool. The hum of animal odor.

Suddenly the pedaling is over.

"The rowing machine next, I think."

They say people have a tendency to fall in love with their shrinks (doctors of the mind); might they also have a tendency to fall in love with their personal trainers (witch doctors of the body)? I have to say it never happened for me. There was no erotic pulse for the testy Swede who would seethe silently as my sit-ups became abdominal white flags. No plucking of the heartstrings for the muscled brunette who would silently (and rather creepily) exercise his own body next to mine. And beautiful though he is, no crashing of violins for this particular trainer, not ever, not even in the beginning. (First Rule of the Female: Never fall in love with a man who intones the word *untoned*.)

Strange though that I always choose male trainers. Or maybe not so strange. Only as strange anyway as the way many women trust only men with their hair. It's as if they perceive women to be so genetically competitive that they cannot be trusted. Though I have yet to hear of female hairstylists going berserk with primitive jealousy and shaving women's hair into Mohawks; or green-eyed lady trainers force-feeding their clients Krispy Kremes on the treadmill.

My reason for choosing male trainers is different (though just as pathetic and inexcusable). I probably thought I could get around them more easily, simper my way out of doing too much, play the cutesy-wootsy girl. A woman would never let you get away with that. But then neither, in my experience, do most male trainers. Certainly there have been times in this guy's company when I have felt less like a woman and more like Richard Gere in *An Officer and a Gentleman*, forced to endless punishment press-ups in the rain; hounded, taunted by the sergeant major until he finally kneels up in the mud, screaming: "I have nowhere else to go!"

"Over here now." The personal trainer wants to move straight on to weights. I scramble to my feet, take a slug of "swimming pool." The entire process takes less than ten seconds. "That's quite enough time-out," he barks, handing me a couple of barbells. "Biceps curls, slow, controlled, thirty each side." (I take them off him, sighing brattishly.) He makes the longest speech of the session: "It's the same every week with you (almost tender), you're only half here, if you don't put more effort in, you won't see any results." "Have you seen *An Officer and a Gentleman*?" "No, why?" "Oh nothing . . . thirty each side, you say?"

Sometimes when I'm pedaling, lunging, or sliding off balls, I get like this—indulging myself in a little cultural counter-sneering at him, and all the rest of the smug buffies, posing around in their Nietzsche-superman Lurex. The way I see it is this: Out of context is out of context. They might be able to do a hundred sit-ups without breaking sweat, but could they discuss the latest Philip Roth? They might have pecs of iron and be able to row at the highest speed, but did they know their Tarantino from their Kaufman? Of course, for all I knew, they could be great on these subjects (and more besides), but I wasn't prepared to give them the benefit of the doubt. At times such as these, you grip tight to your scraps of intellect, your measly crumbs of cultural nous.

All the time knowing that it just doesn't work that way.

The brain might be the most important sexual organ, but does anybody care? Men do not nudge each other lasciviously and say, "I bet she knows her New Order from her Goldfrapp." They don't blow long whistles, thinking: "I wouldn't kick her out of bed for reading Iris Murdoch." Even a very pretty face can come a poor second to the main event—the Bod. If pretty faces mattered that much Kirstie Alley would be an international sex symbol, and the tabloids wouldn't care if she piled it on or off. And nobody would be bitching about poor gammon-armed Britney, trying to get through her career lull the best way she can—getting serially pregnant, and sitting at the car wheel mindlessly munching her way through bumper bags of Doritos.

I think the personal trainer knows this. That's probably why he feels he can get away with doing what he does; What, after all, we ask him to. *It's for their own good*, he thinks, smiling his beautiful smile, stroking his cappuccino skin. *I am doing a great job pointing out to them all how out of shape they are.*

But, as we come to the end of our session, I wonder, is it, is he?

Because I am no longer too thin, because I am not even in the same flesh galaxy as size zero, I admit I'm panicking slightly, here in the chill of Beyond-Youth. Too thin never impressed me much, but now that it has gone, it feels weird. How did it come to this—paying strange men 40 pounds a time to bully me? Deeper than that. Like most women, I have times when I'm sorely in need of a positive reflection. Here at the gym, all I seem to be getting is a hall of mirrors, warped glass, at best a kaleidoscope of random (substandard) body parts (glutes, abs, biceps). Woman once whole, now shattered by toffee hammer. There has to be more out there somewhere. (I know, I have always known, this is not my world.)

"See you next week then," says the trainer, smiling briefly, scribbling something on his clipboard. Maybe, maybe not. It depends on whether I have nowhere else to go.

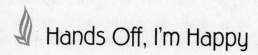

Hands Off, I'm Happy

Julie Burchill

The sad transformation of the word *pamper* goes to show how much pleasure, especially for women, has been pathologized in recent years. Pampering would once have indicated a lost weekend of champagne, lobster, and sodomy; it now means, when used in the context of women, "having a wash" or, perhaps, "keeping the equipment in order."

What it means now is having your hands, feet, thighs, and upper body pulled, poked, and pummeled; oiled, anointed, and scented, so your disgusting female body won't seem quite so disgusting to your unlucky husband/boyfriend when he makes a deposit. Hey, the poor guy's already had to reconcile himself to the fact that he's not having regular penetrative sex with Angelina Jolie; the least you can do is get your cuticles knocked into decent shape!

For, surely, "pampering" is a sad, shop-bought imitation of

the way good sex is supposed to make you feel: relaxed, treasured, confident. You have to hand it to the ingenuity of the marketplace—it knows it can sell sex to men purely as sex, but to women, being the delicate flowers they are, it has to sell it as being clean. In my bleak, dystopian moments, I imagine the twenty-somethings of 2020, the men all shut up in their bedrooms downloading hard-core porn and the women taking long baths in ready-mixed aromatherapy oils called Sensual and Erotic. For many women, titivating themselves has become not a prelude to sex but an end in itself. After all, the last thing you want when you've spent hours honing yourself to perfection is some smelly man putting his greasy mitts on the goods.

The New Narcissists may kid themselves that they're ultra-femme females but, as surely as any cloistered nun, they are dedicated to something far beyond romantic love. Female narcissism is the feminism of the stupid—and it would be better for everyone if it was the only kind of self-regard we were interested in, apparently. Earlier this month, one half of the *Daily Mail*'s front page screamed "Pamper Yourself," offering 30 pounds' worth of moisturizer, aromatherapy oils, bath foam, and scented candles to readers ("The perfect antidote to today's stressful lifestyle"), while the other labored under the headline "Anger Over Astonishing New Right to Abortion." Obviously no one at the paper saw the funny side of this—a stressful lifestyle will obviously not be much improved by the addition of an unwanted child. And you try spending a bit of decent me-time in the tub with a brat screaming next door.

As women have, on average, fifteen hours a week less than

men to devote to leisure, it's rather sad that the little spare
time they do have is consumed by the business of maintaining their market value. Every girl grows up with the mindless
mantra "cleanse, tone, moisturize," but these days this is only
the beginning of any decent skin "regime." The word invari-
ably used to make vacuous primping seem like an outward-
bound course; now you need to masque, exfoliate, polish too.
Twenty years ago, a jar of Nivea cream would cover a multi-
tude of skins, but now there are distinct lotions and potions
for every single bit of the body—eyes, thighs, insteps. I'm
sure that somewhere in a laboratory in Switzerland a clever
scientist is this very moment dreaming up a cream to be used
on some newly discovered essential zone; the two big toes,
perhaps, or the inside of the elbow. And this time next year,
we'll wonder how we ever lived without it.

Even weirder is the growing popularity of the spa holiday,
where the usual two weeks of sea, sun, and sangria are sac-
rificed in favor of seaweed wraps and protein shakes. On a
recent holiday to an all-inclusive resort in Jamaica, the hotel
presented me with a coupon to have whatever I wanted done
at its state-of-the-art spa. From speaking to the other broads,
I understood that they were queuing up to have mud slapped
all over them. I, on the other hand, didn't get there until the
last day, when the girls who worked there expressed real as-
tonishment that I should have preferred to spend the previ-
ous six days lying in the sun with my boyfriend, drinking free
cocktails and generally living it up.

They were lovely to look at, but there was something inert
about them (as there often is about people who are in great

physical shape), something fatally unimaginative that regarded beauty as far superior to, and completely separate from,
fun in general and sex in particular.

Spas may be laughable when they allude to sex—Bliss,
Completely Bare—but they are downright offensive when
their names imply that white Western women are carrying a
burden that weighs them down so singularly that the poor little
diddumses can only bear it by forking out huge sums to have
hot stones placed on their poor broken bodies—Nurturing
Nest, the Sanctuary, Urban Retreat.

The one other time I went to a spa—the Treatment Rooms
in Brighton—strictly for journalistic purposes, I couldn't help
feeling what an indignity it was for a beautiful young girl such
as Sarah to be washing the hideously deformed (if sweet-
smelling) feet of an old lush like me. But when I mentioned
this to a friend who regularly has treatments, she laughed.
"Oh, they love doing it!" Yeah, right; almost as much as hook-
ers love laboring over the smelly parts of all-too-imperfect
strangers too, I bet.

Women always wonder why men do the somewhat nasty
things women are always accusing them of. That is, why they
flee from commitment, why they live in septic pits, why their
idea of fun is smearing pizza on their sheets and drinking la-
ger from their socks, why they wallow in onanism and brute
sports and downloading barnyard porn. It's because they have,
at some point, come into contact with the sort of woman who
frequents spas. And they have decided that any way of being
is better than being like that, even if it makes you Stig of the
Dump.

The Very Angry Homeopath

SUZANNE MOORE

My business these days is the manufacture of mucus. That is what I do. Yes, there is the job and the kids and all the rest of it but what preoccupies me is how much gunk fills up my head. I am full of phlegm. It will not kill me (I realize that) but I do not feel the least phlegmatic about it.

I should perhaps accept that this is a common problem and one that is on the rise. The doctor barely looks at me. "Hay fever. I am seeing a lot of it now." But there is no one making hay in this city. I do not have a fever. For the first time I genuinely cannot have sex because I have a headache. More worrying still is the idea of introducing yet more bodily fluids into the vat of slime I feel myself to be. I am repellent.

The antihistamines come with promises of drowsiness and the inability to drive and manage heavy machinery, inabilities I already possess, even drug-free. Instead, though, I am strangely wired and unable to sleep. No one dies from hay fever, even though I am being smothered into a shadow of my former self.

At the bus stop I see someone I used to know. She asks me how I am and I drone on about how ill I feel. She says it must be awful.

"It is. But how are you?" I ask, benign, saintly almost, considering my obviously distressing predicament.

"Not great actually. Mike has lung cancer."

There is a long wait for the bus while I fumble for tissues to blow my nose.

I never used to have hay fever. It has crept up on me over the years. I blame childbirth. I blame most things on childbirth. Someone once told me that having a baby had the same effect on the body as having a major car accident. This I find peculiarly reassuring, and repeat this incantation as much as possible. "Two years it takes to recover," I mutter darkly to anyone with a swollen belly. I have no idea if this is true or not but it feels true. I didn't have "allergies" before. I didn't even believe in them. Not only do I now have hay fever, if stung by a wasp I turn gangrenous, if I go near a bivalve—even a little clam in a spaghetti vongole—I do spectacular projectile vomiting.

Naturally, someone helpful—a friend even, though I hate everyone at the moment—suggests homeopathy. Homeopathy, the cure for worried well, the placebo for the pleasantly deceived. The treatment for little eczema and asthma, the pampered sprogs of the chronically organic middle classes.

These are not such bitter pills to swallow.

"It can't do any harm."

"No, it can't. Because it hasn't got anything in it. Not one molecule of any decent drug. Nada."

My sole homeopathic experience was not good. One of the children was ill and there was up the road an emergency homeopathic clinic. It was cheap and I was wild for help because antibiotics now appeared to be against the law. I bashed in there with the pushchair. No one opened the door for me, a dingly-dangly dream catcher thing fell on my daughter's head, and she started screaming. Some quietly spoken woman with a bun told me there was a very long wait. I could only quiet the yelling child with a packet of prawn cocktail crisps. I may as well have just given her a crack pipe.

So Annette was not quite what I expected. She was well dressed, for a start. Good shoes. Nice legs. I told her from the start that I was a skeptic. "Ah, skeptics are my favorite people to treat. I always get the best results. I like to work in quite a holistic fashion if that's all right with you."

She then proceeded to ask me many, many questions. About every cold I had ever had, about my family, about how I nearly did but didn't have my tonsils out, about what colors I liked around me, about the position I slept in, whether I preferred rain or snow, how music affected me. She asked whether I was neat. If I was afraid of snakes or dogs. Did I like to have my feet sticking out of the blankets? We talked about my mother. What qualities did I dislike in other people? This, apart from myself, is my favorite subject. As I talked she took notes, she consulted books. God, I have had babies with people less interested in me than she was. This was fantastic. She was, she said, making a timeline.

An hour went past. Maybe more. Annette was not bored by my witterings. She was annotating them. I was feeling better already. What with being so utterly fascinating and everything.

Then I came to.

"The thing is, surely . . . it's just, like, a pollution thing, really, isn't it? That's why more and more people are getting hay fever?"

"Is that what you really think?" she said, uncrossing her legs.

"Uh . . . ? Yeah."

"So why are you here?"

"Well, nothing else works. I suppose I'm fed enough up to give this a go."

"Well, I can help you, but of course you can only heal yourself. It seems to me we are dealing with a lot of shadow energy here and that is why you feel so blocked. We all tend to project our shadows and then hate those people that we have projected them onto. Your symptoms can only be treated if we find the right remedy so that you can take back the shadow. Reintegrate that part of yourself."

"Hey, it's just hay fever, right? Why are we getting into this?"

"I did explain I work holistically."

"Yes but I didn't come for *this*. I came because I can't stop bloody sneezing. Oh look, I am sorry I'm just so irritable all the time at the moment."

"That is obvious, and in your situation perfectly normal. As I said at the beginning, you are perfectly free to see another practitioner, but I happen to think the fear of anger often causes these types of allergies."

"Really I am not angry. Just pissed off."

"You seem to have certain resentments. Nux vomica can help you with that, but it's my professional opinion that you might need more than that. We don't just treat the symptoms. We treat the cause."

"But I like being angry. Anger is an energy. You know . . . John Lydon."

"Who is John Lydon?"

"You don't know? Wow! I just don't want to be so snotty."

"And what do you think snotty really means?"

"Oh just give me the drugs. Or the pretend drugs. Whatever."

Annette very carefully and neatly wrote a prescription for pills that I must on no account touch with my own filthy hands. She had somehow annoyed me intensely. Yet I had liked being able to talk about myself nonstop for an hour and a half. She said I could phone her at any time and should come back in a week.

"What? Should I call you when I am particularly bunged up?" I asked sarcastically. Still, my feeling was she had really enjoyed the challenge. Of me.

I did phone her up when I got home. It was an answering machine but I communicated my gratitude to a tediously welcoming message. Grudgingly.

After all, I had not dismissed her out of hand and I was weirdly looking forward to the next appointment. The following week Annette herself seemed rather sniffly. She even sneezed a couple of times while I was talking about how no one took me seriously enough at work, which was off-putting. She looked less put together, rather disheveled even. For some reason I had dressed up for the occasion.

At one point when I was talking about a particularly bad bout of flu and how the doctor wouldn't do anything about it, she didn't appear as interested as she had at first and kept looking out the window.

"Am I boring you?" I asked, genuinely wanting to know.

"The question is really what boredom means to you."

"Well, you know if you are bored or not, surely? What do you want me to talk about apart from my colds?"

"Your mother."

Something came up into the back of my throat.

Annette looked satisfied now, alert. She got out her notes.

"I couldn't help noticing when I was constructing your timeline that these symptoms started to increase shortly after the death of your mother."

"I just don't know what you mean."

"Well. It was quite striking to me that you talked of her death but not of your grief. Somehow I feel you are still punishing yourself. And also others."

Others? I was mystified.

"But now I am sorry. Our time is up."

I left the consulting room fuming. How dare she? My mum was dead. Cancer of course. Probably because she too didn't "deal" with her anger, didn't have enough candles and relaxation tapes and purple crystals. The sign on the door advertised Annette's services as that of being an "Alternative GP."

You cow, I thought, *you are an alternative. To a real GP*.

Nonetheless, I got more remedies and dutifully tried to get the pills into my mouth without touching them. I regarded it as a waste of time but I didn't feel any different and took to going round in dark glasses and putting Vaseline up my nose.

Mostly though I wanted to see Annette again and put her right. How cheap could these "healers" be? You tell them something meaningful, something true, and they drain it of actual significance and turn it into a bloody symptom to fit their stunted view. What did she know about my grief for my mother? How I had grieved for her before she was dead in that long year when she lay waiting. How we had rowed so much that even toward the end nurses used to have to come and tell us to keep it down . . . but that this was her. Her life-force. What did she know of the times I had to leave her to come back on the train for work and how toward the end I would seek out families with small children, the noisier, the naughtier the better. Signs of life after the metallic smell of radiotherapy. Then for the first time in my life I enjoyed the small talk at parties because it was a relief from the big talk. Of how long. How much more? Which organs are failing? The Ray Charles song she wanted at her funeral, "Take These Chains from My Heart."

How dare this charlatan talk to me about my grieving? As she sat composed, opposite me at the next appointment, I could barely contain myself. Her calmness disgusted me. Her eyes looked swollen but she was still acting the doctor. I was no longer patient.

"I am not better. In fact you have made it worse. Those stupid pills are sugar and I hate the way you ask about my mother. You know nothing about her. About me."

"This is part of the process. I expected that you would direct some of these feelings at me. This is all part of the shadow energy coming toward the surface. But I am here to absorb it, work with it. That is what I can do."

So it was all about her now, was it? Should I just call it a day? Could you sack a spiritual healer? For this woman seemed to be more than a homeopath. It was like going to a vet and then someone telling you they were, by the way, also a gynecologist.

"Did your mother make you feel invisible?"

Jesus, I wanted to slap the living daylights out of her. Right here in this deliberately muted room with its carefully chosen pictures that could never offend or excite anybody.

"I am sensing your difficulties with that question."

"Just let's stop the mother thing. You don't know anything about it. That's not what I came here for."

"In my experience the reasons people give for coming to see me are never the reasons they are actually here."

"What? I can't win? I hate this."

Annette smiled, really smiled at me for the first time.

"It's not this you hate. It's not me you hate, is it? Why don't you say what it is?"

So I did.

I ranted on about how I hated people who thought they knew me, or knew more than me, and people who never listened and for whom I was never good enough.

"And people who think they have all the answers . . . like you."

"I don't claim to know or be any of those things. This is simply what you choose to assume about me. Can we perhaps get back to your original symptoms? Are they easing at all?"

"My snottiness? Oh no. It's still there. Great gallons of it. My eyes won't stop streaming. I look like I have been crying forever."

"And have you?"

"No! I can't help it. It's bloody hay fever. Pollen. Crap."

"But crying? Is it possible you have not cried enough in your life? You must listen to what your body is saying."

"Christ, Annette, you are not listening to me." I walked out. The door slammed. This was a big noise in a place where lost souls were being silently Reikied and rubbed, massaged and manipulated.

"Is everything all right?" inquired the startled and startlingly posh receptionist.

"No. Because if it was you couldn't run this business, could you?"

The assembled throng of the worried well patients looked up disapprovingly, as though there really was something wrong with me.

That night Annette called me at home. She said she really wasn't used to having "clients" walk out in the middle of a session, that she was not only deeply concerned about me but also felt that she deserved better treatment. She suggested we meet somewhere outside the "therapeutic space." All this she said in such an urgent manner, as though without such dramatic intervention I might do something stupid.

We agreed to meet in one of those fashionable delis whose café served only the vaguest approximations of things you might want. Coffee made out of dandelions, cakes made out of everything except what you need to actually make a cake. I waited an hour for her but she didn't turn up.

So now I got it. I had walked out on her and she had punished me for it.

She wanted a piece of my mind. Or a piece of the mind/body continuum, and she was bloody well going to have it.

"So let's start again then." She forced a smile when I reappeared in her room. But she looked awful, blotchy and tired.

"What about the other day. You weren't there. How can we start again?"

"I was simply demonstrating to you how you make others feel. How you make other people hold you in their minds and then blame them for caring. How undermining that can be. And I wonder who that might remind you of."

"I have got hay fever."

"And how is it?"

"My head is going to burst. Explode right here. Over your Tibetan prayer flags. You know, I can't take any more of this shadow rubbish. What you do, it doesn't work. What you say, it doesn't make sense. And ever since I have been coming here you go on and on about me being angry but you are the one that sits there all smug and hostile. You are the one playing games, not me."

"What you decide is up to you. I don't know if you even realize that you have expected me to absorb a huge amount of what we shall have to agree to call negative energy. You have constantly belittled me, told me that what I do here is worthless and that my experience counts for nothing."

Had I said that? I had merely thought it, surely? Which was different. Wasn't it?

"I regard part of my work as trying to forgive in others what they cannot forgive in themselves. For this I may be the scapegoat for the shadow energy, but usually this is a project I embark on *together* with my clients.

"With you I am aware that the original scapegoat was indeed driven out into the woods, where it was killed and its energy was, shall we say . . . neutralized."

"This is your stuff. This is not about me. You don't even see who I am . . ."

"Don't I? Trust me, I am more than conscious of my failure with you. Indeed so much so that I feel my own shadow has risen to the surface. So it is probably best that we end the treatment *right now*."

She was actually shouting at me.

"What? What if I don't want to? Doctor?"

"As you have reminded me several times I am not what you call a proper doctor. And I would like you to leave now before I do something I will regret."

"Are you threatening me?"

"Yes."

"But I am not . . . like . . . cured."

I stumbled out of that room. The sun was dazzling and the sneezing started. I couldn't quite believe it. She had totally lost it. How unprofessional. As the day went on, though, I started to brighten up. A glass of wine didn't make my head dull. My eyes stopped running. The pollen count must have dropped dramatically. I put on one of my mother's rings. Our hands were the same size. She had fine hands. So did I. Like with like. What a fucking bitch that woman turned out to be. I felt so much better.

Q&A with Susie Essman

A veteran of the New York stand-up circuit, Susie Essman is best known as the foul-mouthed Susie Greene on HBO's Curb Your Enthusiasm. *Susie has become a favorite character on* Curb *as the manifestation of a female who never tries to repress or internalize her rage. She is in the great tradition of glam vulgarians, like Joan Rivers and Tina Fey, who hit you with a one-two punch. First she shocks you with the bare, foul-mouthed truth; then she shocks you again because the foul mouth isn't bare at all, but juicily clad in lip gloss. Like Lucille Ball and Mary Tyler Moore, she is both pretty and funny and fans who come to her stand-up show are often flummoxed by that:*

SE: "But "You're so much prettier in real life!" Or, "You're so much thinner in real life!" What I get most is, "You're so much smaller and prettier and younger than you look on TV." So in other words, I'm fat and ugly on television where millions of people are watching me. That feels really good.

EF: I saw you had lots of interesting MAC lipglosses back-stage.

SE: When I'm performing live, my warm-up begins with putting on my makeup. I try not to wear it all day and if I have had makeup on I usually take it off and start from scratch. Not that it's all that elaborate of a process but it's putting on my game face and so it begins. I don't know where I go in my head and I have no idea how I get there, but I do know that putting on my makeup is the first step. A couple of hours later I end up on stage in an altered state, a zone. My ritual makeup application is my cue to focus and begin my prayers to the humor gods.

EF: And you have good fancy curly hair products in your bathroom, I noticed. You know we have two essays in the book about coping with curly hair.

SE: When it comes to film and television, I can't tell you how many times I've been asked to straighten my hair. My hair seems to scare the shit out of people. I have yet to figure out what's so threatening about my curly mane but there is definitely some ethnic component. I'm a comedian for God's sake, not a newscaster! And yet I've been in meeting after meeting where it's all about my hair. Believe me, nobody's going to mistake me for some WASP from Indiana just because I've gotten a good blowout.

EF: The execs are Jewish men and they're not attracted to Jewish women.

SE: Right, they run for the hills. My theory? We remind them of their mothers. Or maybe it's all those Jewish girls in camp and school who were smarter than them and made them feel inadequate and out of control. Either way, it's unconscious payback. I don't think the audiences across the country think about it all that much. You either make them laugh or not. But the guys in charge? Maybe the curly hair is simply symbolic of a wild mind and big mouth that can't be tamed or controlled.

EF: I always think it's crazy that in America women's dress size goes down to a size zero. And actresses compete for that size, as if they're trying to take up as little space, physically and emotionally, as possible.

SE: The visual for women today is a reflection of the political atmosphere we're living in. All these skinny girls out there right now? These big-headed, emaciated, scary-looking girls? What's the message? Don't look like a woman. Don't have hips and flesh and boobs. Real women are scary. They have the ultimate power. They create life. Who can compete with that?

EF: Well that's not just Hollywood, that's also the world's religions.

SE: It's not by chance that the world is dominated by the religions that seem to find women threatening. Orthodox Jewish men say a prayer every morning thanking God for not making them a woman. The Islamic fundamentalists are so threatened by women that they keep them completely covered and unable to express themselves visually, let alone learn to read and write. The argument that women should only be seen and desired by their husbands is disingenuous. It's one more way to keep women powerless and at the mercy of men. The Catholics tell women that the only reason to have sex is to procreate. The underlying message is that women who like sex are whores. Jerry Falwell claims that the gays were responsible for hurricane Katrina. The only thing more threatening than a woman, it seems, is a man who acts like a woman. In fact, they're so threatening that they can destroy entire cities! Keeping a woman in her place is an old political ploy that's been used for thousands of years. And it's smart. These guys are no dummies. Our sexual desires are some of our most base and primordial instincts. They have to be. Species that are uninterested in sex will become extinct very quickly. What better way to control people than to tell them that their deepest most natural desires are bad or wrong? Control people's sexual behavior and you have power.

EF: So is it truly possible to be a lipstick feminist? To go crazy at MAC and still be a good feminist?

SE: Look, in some societies a lipstick is a powerful political symbol. Makeup and adornment are some of the oldest forms of human expression. Beauty and politics mix. They are in many ways inseparable. I particularly like makeup companies like MAC and Revlon that support women's causes. It is, after all, a billion-dollar business, so there's a vested interest in keeping us all happy and healthy. After all, altruism is political too.

The Dark Side of Reflexology

ELLEN KARSH

I make no secret of my fear of tumors—of life-threatening illnesses in general—and of people with any kind of training at all who may intentionally or unintentionally discover them. I don't go for physical examinations, for facials, for tummy tucks, for acupuncture, for deep tissue massage. I rarely even get a flu shot. I run out of restaurants during dinner when customers at neighboring tables compare their intestinal blockages or painful joints or irritable bowels. I hold my ears when "mild gas pains" and "ovarian cancer" are used in the same sentence. Therefore, it came as a complete and unwelcome surprise when a friend gave me a gift certificate (it wasn't even my birthday) for a session with her reflexologist.

"Your feet will love reflexology, even if you don't," she said (hesitantly), as she handed me the envelope. "You'll feel the stress and anxiety ooze out of you the second the reflexologist's hands touch your big toe."

While I didn't know much about reflexology at the time, I knew enough about *me* to know that my feet would not love a person who has been trained to recognize which part of the insteps or arches are linked in some ominous way to the colon and the spleen.

I tried to look grateful and open-minded. "I'll make the appointment," my friend offered, "just in case you get cold *feet*. And quit looking so horrified—she's a *reflexologist,* not a gastroenterologist."

I didn't see much difference between the two.

Fortunately, the reflexologist couldn't squeeze me into her clogged schedule for a full ten days, giving me plenty of time to bone up on reflexology.

I read articles, papers, transcripts of speeches. I read websites and press releases. And I learned that nothing—not even a total-body MRI, if there is such a thing—could offer more possibilities for digging up diseases than an hour stretched out on a reflexologist's recliner. Although reflexology is known for its soothing ambience, it didn't take much reading between the lines for me to realize that the reflexologist—ambience or no ambience—is palpating the feet like mad for sixty nonstop minutes and is bound to see what havoc is being wreaked throughout the body.

Reflexology is no ordinary foot massage.

If the pancreas or liver or kidneys are diseased and about to shut down, the reflexologist will know it.

The small and large intestines! The heart! The brain! From

what I understand, they are all specialties of the reflex-ologist.

With my appointment looming, I had to confront—for the millionth time—my illness-obsessed history, which I have dis-cussed at great length (and at great expense) with perplexed therapists who have, thus far, been unable to cure me of my photographic memory of every symptom, no matter how mi-nor, I have ever heard about that turned out to be something horrific.

The momentary double vision that turned out to be MS.

The headache that turned out to be a subdural hematoma.

The sniffles that turned out to be Hodgkin's disease.

The minute I feel a twinge (and who doesn't get shoot-ing pains knifing through their body every so often?), I re-member, like a computer doing a Google search, every pos-sible fatal thing it could be. Stiff neck? I don't assume it was caused by sleeping in an awkward position. I instantly land on spinal cancer, the symptoms of which I can dredge up in a heartbeat. Bellyache? Hand pain? Oddly shaped blemishes in unexpected locations? I instantly remember that someone at work was once diagnosed with cancer of the appendix, some-one else with cancer of the palm of her hand. And where on the body—the inner thigh, the wrist, the thumb—hasn't a deadly melanoma been known to sprout?

The night before my feet were scheduled to come into con-tact with the reflexologist's perceptive fingers, I remembered reading about a masseuse in the Midwest who found a micro-scopic lump that turned out to be lymphoma embedded deep in the back muscles of a supposedly healthy mother of twins.

One minute the mom was taking a few relaxing hours away from the kids having her back and shoulders massaged with sweet-smelling creams; the next minute, it was chemotherapy and a bad prognosis.

I'm not sure why I get myself so worked up. I'm not only petrified that illnesses will be detected in shocking ways, I'm also deathly afraid of actually being sick. I could just be a born worrier the way other people are born optimists—but there are possible psychological causes.

My father was a hypochondriac; he spent much of his adult life thinking he was in cardiac arrest. He once ran into the street completely naked because a neighbor called him on the telephone and said I was carrying a glass jar and he was afraid I'd break it and sever a vein. That wasn't the act of a hypochondriac but it was typical of the extreme health-related behavior I was regularly exposed to when I was young. (Following in my father's footsteps, I drove friends crazy because I was convinced that my doctor—I had a routine physical examination before I left on a trip to Europe after college—was trying to track me down in the Zurich airport to tell me I had leukemia and needed to hurry home for blood transfusions.)

One of my earliest childhood memories is of being awakened by the excruciating prick of a penicillin injection in the middle of the night—pediatricians made house calls back then and neither doctors nor parents saw the need to wake children up and actually explain to them what was about to happen to their backsides. My mother only recently admitted that for years after the injection, I threw a tantrum whenever I saw anyone in a white coat—even if it was worn by the cheerful man who sold ice cream from his truck.

Not surprisingly, I have an actual rare condition—white coat hypertension—that causes my blood pressure to spiral wildly out of control in a doctor's office (and, probably, in a reflexologist's office—even if the reflexologist is not wearing a white coat). Years ago, my gynecologist wouldn't let me leave her office without a prescription for a beta-blocker because she was sure that, unmedicated, I would burst a blood vessel in my brain on the subway heading home. She frightened me so much that I agreed to wear a twenty-four-hour blood pressure monitor, the results of which revealed that my pressure skyrockets only when I'm around doctors, not when I'm, say, around lawyers.

Now, except for this unexpected reflexology appointment, I stay far away from people who are going to examine (even if they don't use that word) me, my blood, my organs, my skin, my muscles, my bones, or my feet. The last straw was a series of alarming test results—I had no symptoms whatsoever— which forced me, finally, to undergo a medical procedure that required me to breathe deeply into a plastic tube for a really long time while crouching in a tiny airless chamber to make sure I wasn't a candidate for a heart-lung machine and a motorized wheelchair. Luckily, the test results were negative— but the gagging, the sweating, the irate technician who kept hollering at me for breathing wrong took a toll.

For as long as I can remember I've tried everything that anyone suggested—and everything that I dreamed up on my own—to tackle my fears. I've tried biofeedback with a certified biofeedback specialist. I've tried deep breathing exercises. I've read books containing strategies to clear the mind, to be self-accepting, to overcome anxiety. (I've even read books about how anxiety itself can kill you.) I've listened to relaxation tapes. I've gone to yoga classes. I've tried reminding myself again and again that aches and pains and blemishes and itches can metastasize into *catastrophic* aches and pains and blemishes and itches the longer no one—whether it be a doctor, a masseuse, a reflexologist—finds them. And I've tried to figure out why none of my friends requires endless hours of psychoanalysis before they can bring themselves to go for endoscopies and CAT scans when they have a little trouble digesting green peppers or swallowing vitamin pills.

I can't go for a neck and shoulder massage at a day spa, let alone for a CAT scan. All the therapies, the exercises, the reading matter, the lectures and warnings I've given myself have been futile.

And now, unfortunately, it was time to face the reflexologist.

In spite of my recent stabs at positive thinking, my unsuccessful attempts to stop picturing the masseuse who discovered lymphoma, my deep breathing exercises with sitar music playing softly in the background, I was ill-prepared for reflexology as I finally made my way uptown to keep my appointment.

The only recollection I have of the reflexologist's office is that she uses her kitchen and dining room as her workspace, which, on the surface, is not very threatening. It's hard to imagine cancer of the appendix being diagnosed at the dining room table or near the kitchen sink.

I have almost no recollection of the reflexologist herself—except that she had excellent posture. I told her that I was fit as a fiddle and healthy as a horse. I did not mention anything about shooting pains knifing through my body, although she asked whether I had any complaints, because I didn't want to motivate her to try to figure out what was causing them.

Sitting in the reflexologist's kitchen, waiting for the procedure to begin, knowing that it was only a matter of time until she'd find something worrisome, I could have been in the emergency room of a hospital—except we were bathed in flickering light from almond-scented candles.

"Shall we begin?" the reflexologist asked, after we chatted about the weather for a few upsetting minutes.

"I'm ready," I said jovially.

I didn't tell her that I was terrified.

I didn't have to.

The minute she touched my feet, I asked, "Do you feel anything?"

"What do you mean?"

"My organs. How are they?"

She smiled and kept doing what she was doing.

Every few minutes I asked her if I seemed to be in good shape, if she was noticing anything surprising. Instead of lying back with my eyes peacefully closed and my mind cleared of all dark thoughts, I sat upright with my eyes wide open and my mind filled with visions of renal failure and bone marrow transplants.

The reflexologist said nothing about my liver, nothing about my lungs, no matter how many times, and in how many ways,

I begged her to tell me what she was feeling as she kneaded my feet.

But her silence and her benign smiles did nothing to reassure me. And even if I could trick myself into believing that cancer or hardening of the arteries or autoimmune diseases were a bit out of the reflexologist's diagnostic range, she *was* prowling around the twenty-six bones and thirty-three joints, as well as the countless muscles and ligaments, of my feet for a solid hour; she could easily have stumbled upon dangerous masses, discolorations, abrasions, infections, and lesions hiding among the bunions and calluses. Even a little puffiness around the ankle can be a sign of something extremely dire!

I thanked the reflexologist profusely when the session was finally over—silently thanking her even more profusely for not suggesting that I immediately make an appointment for a barium enema or a thyroid workup or a spinal tap.

I told her that I could practically see the anxiety and stress ooze out of me the minute she touched my big toe. I told her that she has magical hands, that I'd like to buy some of the oil she used, that my generous and wise friend really knew a perfect gift to give a person like me, that I loved her kitchen appliances, her linoleum, and the color of her walls.

I practically gave her a big kiss on the cheek.

What I neglected to mention, of course, is that I don't have the stomach for reflexology—that I can't believe I survived the session without having a myocardial infarction or a stroke—and that I will never force my poor, nervous feet to undergo such scrutiny again.

 Hair Rage

MARIAN KEYES

Hair rage: emotion. Feeling generated by hairstylists, when they willfully mishear requests, spitefully misinterpret photographs, bouff you when you specifically requested no bouffing, and generally send you out into the world with terrible hair.

4:58 P.M.

Arrive at salon (fancy one on Fifth Avenue, for what it's worth) for five P.M. appointment. First mistake. Never arrive early. Or on time. Always be late. They respect that; you are playing their game. To arrive early is to invite shit treatment.

State my business to dopey receptionist called Organza (at least that is what name badge says). "I have appointment with Redwood for blow-dry."

"Redwood is just finishing up." She directs me to waiting area.

"How long will he be?" I ask boldly.

She, looking aghast at my temerity, "Just a few minutes."

I see. Just a few minutes. But am on Hair Time now. And Hair Time behaves differently from time in any other part of the universe. Syndrome has actually been studied by prominent physicists and devastating discovery made: Within confines of hair salon, time slows down—oh yes—and stretches to elastic, groany lengths. "Five minutes" takes twenty minutes to elapse, "two tics" equates to eight and a half minutes and "just finishing up" is unquantifiable.

"Niagara will see you now," of *particular* interest to physicists because unlike rest of universe, which exists in perpetual, recurring state of "now," "now" cannot exist within walls of salon. Instead, "now" exists in continuous state of deferment and is defined as *any time other than now.*

Indeed, the time your stylist will see you becomes a Self-Canceling Event. It can only occur *at any time other than the time you booked for.*

Just one event will cause time to contract within salon: when costly deep-conditioning treatment is applied to hair. Although it should stay on hair for ten minutes, the ten minutes will magically elapse in two and you will be rinsed despite protests that it's only just been put on.

5:01 P.M.

Sit in waiting area with six other women. Anxious.

5:07 P.M.

People who have arrived later than me have been taken

away to be washed. Has happened twice. Have grudge against them.

5:13 P.M.

Wonder what time it is. Swotty internal Virgo timekeeper tells me have been here twelve minutes, forty-five seconds, but am better off not having that confirmed. Profound realization: Reason I never wear watch is because if could chart minute-by-minute lateness of every appointment have ever had in hairdresser's, might kill someone.

5:14 P.M.

Espy Redwood! (Beautiful, shaven-headed black man who looks like he could star in modern-dance production of *Ferris Bueller's Day Off* but that is neither here nor there.) He is cutting some other woman's hair! And doesn't look like he'll be finished any time soon! Do speedy calculation. Another ten minutes on cutting, fifteen on blow-drying, another two on pointless strand-moving, then another three to five for the business with the second mirror to display wonders of back of hair, and that will mean it will be five-forty-five before he even raises his dryer for me.

Panic starts upward spiral. Am used to hair delays, but today it matters. Am having launch party for new novel at seven P.M. Big, glitzy deal in fancy place, with many, many invitees. In such circumstances, should have made hair appointment for much earlier but am just in from promo work in Boston. This was best I could manage. And now will be late! Late for own party! Dreadful Virgo voice-in-head with stopwatch means I hate being late for anything, but for own party! The rude-ness! Also the fear! New York media folk impatient people. Have eighteen other parties to go to. If am not there when they arrive, they won't stick around. Career opportunity up in flames!

Approach Organza. Tell her what have seen with own eyes: Redwood tied up for next twenty-five minutes. Implication: I am smarter than you think, Organza.

"Can someone else do me?" I ask.

Slowly she turns her eyes downward to the book and begins to scan. But all around us other people are shouting. "Organza, stall my five-fifteen! Get her a free treatment!" "Organza, I've got roots! You need to take away my roots!" "Organza, have waited ten minutes and am leaving! You tell Charlemaine from me that his mother sucks big elephant dicks!"

Organza looks up from book, as though coming around from bad blow to head. She watches all the people yelling at her, as though she can see them but not hear them, as though they are just many mouths opening and contorting and closing.

Profound realization: Hair salon receptionists may not be—as had thought up until now—cretinously stupid. In-stead, perhaps are operating in state of emotional lockdown, barely daring to engage with the world around them, because the stress would cause heart to seize up in chest.

"Me, you were talking to me," I say. So often, become invis-ible in hair salon. (Other syndrome for physicist looking for subject for tenure paper to study.)

"Oh yeah." She finally sees me. "No one else can do you. But Redwood will be just a few minutes. He'll be right with you."

"He won't. He's cutting someone else's hair. He'll be another half hour."

"No, he's really fast. Just a few more minutes."

"Look," I say. "This is really important. I've a party to go to."

"I've got a party too," another client chimes in. Closer examination shows she is woman who told Organza to tell Charlemaine that his mother sucks big elephant dicks. She is still here? Had admired her storming-out chutzpah, but looks like she is just all talk.

"Me too, I've a party too." (Roots woman.)

"Yes," I say, "but it's *my* party. To launch my new book."

This sort of information might have carried weight in One Horse, Wisconsin, but this is Fifth Avenue, Manhattan.

"What's your name?" Implication was clear. If I was famous enough, Organza would help me out.

"Norman Mailer."

"Who?"

"OK, Jackie Collins." Surely she'd heard of her?

"You're not Jackie Collins," she says slowly.

"No, you're right, am not."

"Redwood'll be right with you."

5:17 P.M.

Return to waiting area. Decide to leave. Will go to party with unclean, unlovely hair. Confidence will be in flitters, all conversations will be held with my dirty hair, but will live with it.

5:18 P.M.

Russian woman called Galina appears before me. Says, "Put on khown. I vill vash."

Hope begins mad, giddy dance. All going to be OK! Redwood *is* very fast! Hair will be blow-dried and beautiful and won't be late for party. ALL GOING TO BE OK!!!

5:19 P.M.

Sit at basin.

5:23 P.M.

Still sitting at basin.

5:24 P.M.

Woman sits at next basin. Has suitcase-sized Birkin bag in taupe crocodile skin.

5:26 P.M.

Galina appears—and washes Birkin bag woman! Me, sitting dry-haired and Birkin-less, belly-wash of bile swilling around in mouth.

5:27 P.M.

Galina leads shampooed and betoweled Birkin bag to outer chamber.

5:28 P.M.

Decide, Fuck this. Am really going this time. Galina reappears, tucking what looks like a $20 bill into her blouse pocket. Says, "Hed to vash other leddy. VIP leddy."

5:29 P.M. to 5:35 P.M.

Galina does shampoo and hairdresser head "massage" which is not massage at all, just rubbing scalp harder than usual. "Rhelex," Galina orders. "Enjoy massage." But cannot. This is not massage, this is stalling mechanism.

5:36 P.M.

Return to waiting area.

5:39 P.M.

Wait.

5:42 P.M.

Continue to wait.

5:45 P.M.

Dawns on me what a terrible mistake it was to get hair washed. Now am trapped. Bad and all as unclean hair was, a self blow-dry would be worse. Frizz. Calf's-lick. More frizz. Shocking.

5:46 P.M.

Lean sideways to check on Redwood's progress—and all becomes slow-motion horror. Redwood is blow-drying some-one. But she's different woman! New woman! Closer look. It's Birkin bag! Have been bumped for Birkin bag!

Momentarily refuse to believe this travesty, this injustice. Am rooted to spot, then rush of hysteria propels me to desk!

"Organza," I say, in trembling, rage-soaked words, "Red-wood's doing someone else!"

"Yeah," she says slowly. "There was other client ahead of you. But he'll just be few minutes."

"She wasn't ahead of me. She wasn't ahead of me! I was NEXT!"

People are looking. Don't care. Let them look. Let them—yes—bear witness to this miscarriage of justice.

"Have been here since five o'clock and it's now—what time is it?" Wildly I cast the question at circle of onlookers.

"Five after six."

"Five past SIX?" I shriek. Longer than I thought. Internal clock has started lying to me. Denial. Saving me from myself. "Five past SIX? If you only knew how important tonight is, how nervous I am, how—"

Mid-rant, attention is caught by short, stout stylist with dreadful straggly gray ponytail, standing halfway across salon. He gestures to me, then points at empty chair at his station.

Me? Pointed at myself and mouthed, Do you mean *me?*

He nodded and I took it all back about his straggly gray ponytail. Saved. Oh, thank you, God, I'm saved!

On trembling legs, lower self into chair and look at him in mirror.

"I'm Viscount," he says.

"Marian."

"You're writer, I hear," he said. "I'm artist myself."

"Good for you." Now please dry my hair.

"Hard call being creative."

"Yes, indeed." Less of the chat now. Just dry my fucking hair.

"Because we're sensitive, sometimes we behave badly. Got it?"

"Got it." Got what? Are you philosopher?

"Good. All righty, up you get, my client is here."

"What . . . ? You mean . . . you're not going to do my hair?"

"Oh no. Was just being a friend."

Can't believe it. Cannot fucking believe it. So much so, stay where I am.

"Up," he repeats, giving the chair a little shake.

And I hate him as have never hated anyone, and believe me, have had plenty of practice. Decide he is not one of those fat people who have slow metabolism or trouble with thyroid. He is fat because he is greedy, angry pig who eats too much. Repeat his stupid name to self: Viscount. Will remember that. Will put him on my List of Enemies. Will put him in pride of place, right at top of list. *Above* the line, in margin right at top of page. Viscount. What sort of name is that?

Profound insight. Reason hairdressers have unlikely names: They are not their real names. They make so many enemies in course of their work that when they leave safety of salon environment every evening, they have to assume entirely different identity—similar to witness protection program—so cannot be hunted down like dogs and suffer hideous death with their own implements—metal combs, bulldog clips, et al.

Redwood in deep discussion with Birkin bag, concerning root bouff, from reading their hand movements. Evidently she is persnickety client and will not be finished any time soon. This is utter nightmare. Tell self that I am not trapped in ore mine in Tasmania with dwindling air supply and no hope of rescue. Or in broken submarine at bottom of freezing ocean off the coast of Kursk. Or in. . .

6:15 P.M.

Cell phone rings—husband calling from hotel to say that car has arrived to take us to party. Mildly hyperventilating, explain situation.

"Leave," he advises. "You can't be late to your own party. Your hair will do."

"Hair is wet." I say. "Must see this through to bitter—oh yes—bitter end."

"No time for you to get back here to change. Tell me what you want to wear tonight and will bring in car to salon. You can change at party."

"Black dress," I gasp. But had fourteen black dresses in hotel room. To uninitiated, they look identical, but to me, they are wholly different and only one of the fourteen would do. Other thirteen were disasters.

Gasping and wheezing like asthmatic, I talk him through it. Listen to much rummaging in suitcases and clattering of hangers in wardrobe. Finally we run Chosen One to ground.

"And wedge sandals. Not ones with wooden soles—"

"—but gold ones. Got them."

"No, no, no! Not gold ones! Christ no! With black dress? Other ones, other ones!"

We discuss underwear, jewelry, and makeup and then hang up, certain have forgotten something.

6:20 P.M.

Begin to cry, openly sobbing with rage, not caring who sees me. Glad—yes glad—that these bastards have to live with evidence of their . . . their . . . treachery, their cruelty.

Suddenly remember every injustice have ever suffered at hands of a hairdresser, every ignored request, every unflattering cut, every hausfrau blow-dry. My hairdressing life flashes before eyes and can't help wondering, am I about to die?

What makes me cry hardest is all the wasted time, the hours and hours frittered away sitting reading *People* in the waiting area. Such futility! Could have learned a skill in that time. Conversational Spanish. Or cake icing. Could have set up own business doing novelty birthday cakes: football pitches for men, handbags for women, Barneys for children. Could have *done* something with my life.

Then am not just weeping for me. Am crying for all those other women who requested golden lowlights "just like in this picture here" and instead got headful of orangey stripes. For every woman who ever said, "Just a trim" and instead got ugly, brutal crop. For every woman who got blow-dry for hot date and left salon feeling less confident than before went in. All the hair injustice in the world flows out through my eyes and I sob and sob and sob.

6:25 P.M.

Make mistake of asking another woman the time. Six-twenty-five! This is unbelievable! Literally unbelievable! Consider fainting with disbelief. Have been here almost hour and half! Hour and half! And no one cares. Wave after wave of shuddery hysteria rises. Am going to be so late. Will get into so much trouble with publicist. After all the money publishers have spent on party and all the hard work bullying people to say they'll come, I will ruin it all by not being there.

Yet another wave of wild panic rises and this time, catch it and ride it. Am on feet before know what am doing and—watched by several startled eyes—I find dryer, pick it up, turn it on, and—yes—start blow-drying hair myself. Response is immediate. Firm hands wrestle dryer from my hands. More firm hands are placed on my shoulders and steer me back to the waiting area, a broken woman.

6:35 P.M.

Viscount, the fat philosopher, appears from nowhere. "Your lucky day! My six-thirty has had to go into rehab. I can take you now."

Although hate him more than life itself, follow him to station and manage to gasp, "Straight. Just straight. Straight bangs, straight length, flat on top."

"Flat on top?"

"Yes, flat." Had to pause to breathe. "No body, no volume, no lift at roots."

Don't want to look like senator's wife in wake of sex-scandal, where they have to do happy-family shot, with kids swinging on the gate. Have been given this look once too often on this book tour and is just not me.

He picks up dryer, switches it on. Am holding breath, expecting power outage, building collapse, or some other impediment. Life starting to feel like episode of *Lost*: suspect satisfaction will never be given, conclusion will never be reached, hair will never be done.

However, to amazement, drying commences, fatso Viscount droning on about his art shows, me doing shuddery, post-hysterical-crying breathing, not even pretending to listen.

7 P.M.
Am now officially late.

7:05 P.M.
Fat philosopher switches off dryer. "There ya go," he says. "Run off and enjoy your little party."

I observe, "My bangs aren't straight." Bangs, in fact, are entirely cylindrical, turned inward and upward, as though wrapped around Twinkie bar. Look ridiculous, like kooky East Village chick, circa 1991. All was missing were polka-dot deely-boppers.

Viscount makes halfhearted attempt with brush to straighten things out, but no improvement.

I remain seated. "No, still not straight." Although very late, had waited this long, *would not leave* with cylindrical bangs. Point of principle.

"Am not going to do them any straighter."

"Why not?"

"Your hair . . . it looks a little . . . wiggy."

" . . . . . . "

"Wiggy," he repeats.

I locate voice. "Wiggy?"

"Yeah. You know. Like a wig. Straighter bangs will only make it worse."

"Can live with it," I say, fury rinsing my mouth. "Straight bangs, as wiggy as you like."

We eyeball each other in mirror, fighting silent battle of wills.

He shrugs, switches on dryer. "It's your funeral."

Within seconds he's turned dryer off again. "Can't do it. Your hair's too tricky."

Tricky, wiggy hair. Thank you, I feel beautiful, like skipping through meadow full of spring flowers, swinging my hair.

7:06 P.M.

He tips me from chair.

"No," I say. "Do the thing with the mirror where you show me back of hair."

"Excuse me?"

I repeat, "The thing with the mirror where you show me back of hair."

Know my rights. Have no interest at all in rear view of hair but refuse to be fobbed off with incomplete service. Point of principle. Yes, another one.

7:07 P.M.

Go to desk. Hand over credit card. Organza gives me slip to add tip.

Wonder—for brief, crazy moment—what would happen if simply left line blank? Would world cease to turn? Would I be reduced to ash by bolt of lightning? Would crack squad of hair avengers track me down and exact terrible revenge? Leave it blank, leave it blank, leave it blank . . .

7:08 P.M.

Temptation was enormous.

7:09 P.M.

But fear was greater.

Picked up pen, swallowed back rage and hatred and urge to write "Fuck you, motherfucker," and wrote in a tip.

PART V

Wax Poetic

SORAYA

Soraya came to America from Iran in 1976. Her specialty is the Playboy wax, which she insists will improve any woman's sex life. Her other specialty is the traditional Persian leg wax, in which she rubs your waxed legs with lemon juice and then seeds to inhibit growth. She "operates" out of her Beverly Hills apartment, where photos of clients Daryl Hannah and Brittany Murphy gaze down on your nakedness.

My whole family came here. Persians like the mountains in California because that's like Iran. But Tehran, where I grew up, is like New York. We have four seasons, hot summer, snow. Iranians are spoiled and they like no matter what season they have to have all kinds of fruit. They want what they want when they want it—like Californians. Iranians want adventure, fun, nothing repeated or boring, we're just fun, fun, fun people.

Genetically, we have really good skin. I'd say seventy percent. It's a good skin all around. I'm fifty-six. I never get a facial. I got one once and it messed up my skin more. As a little girl in Tehran, we didn't have hot water in the house. Instead we went every Friday to, like, a spa, where you go spend all day? You get these units, then someone comes in and they do a strong loofah to get all the dead skins out of you. All this dead skin like crazy. You do that once a week. Then the same person would scrub your legs, then wash your hair. I hated it because when they washed your hair, God they would be so rough.

You know waxing came from Egypt hundreds of years ago? In Iran you have full body wax day before your wedding. Wax everywhere. Whole day. I used to work out of an office but now I work from home, which is good, because it's a very intimate process. Coming to my home, it's more comfortable for the client. Women aren't self-conscious about taking off their panties for me. They are more aware now, compared to ten years ago. If you want a good wax, a detailed job . . . you have to take your underwear off.

I do men's initials down there. I do arrows. I do such a clean job. It makes the guy feel special. Men get so spoiled. Woman need to understand that they must do it for themselves. Not for the man. You feel so clean, and have so much more confidence. And you can feel sexy. And enjoy sex more.

The youngest client is fifteen years old. The oldest in her sixties. I have clients that come all the way up until the last week of their pregnancy, so they feel good about themselves when they deliver.

I don't feel weird about seeing so many different vaginas. Everybody is different. So what? I do a good job. There is a lot of bad waxing out there. A lot of waxers out there use a honey-based wax . . . and it's mostly oil. Bad. Bad! The wax can actually come out of your pores. Bad. The oil gets in, blocks the pores, and causes so many ingrown hairs.

When you are lying on Soraya's bed, there is a beautifully framed drawing hanging above the waxing table that says "Welcome Amerie," with a cartoon face of a man in spectacles with his tongue hanging out.

The story is I was in Bangkok. They took us to this sex show. The only place where you find the strongest muscles of the pussy are in Bangkok. These women can throw darts from their vaginas. They can open Coke bottles with these muscles. They opened a bottle I couldn't even open with my hand!

The last woman they showed, she stuck a marker pen up inside herself. She took off the top, and squatted to almost the floor, and she wrote a welcome picture to our tour. The cartoon is the drawing of our tour guide from this trip. It looks *exactly* like him. I told them I had to have it!!!

And so now that's what my clients get to look at while I'm busy at work down there.

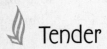 Tender

MARCELLE KARP

It hits me the first time I see her: She's a traumatic vision.

Look at her. Ginger Spice red hair pulled tight into two hanging doornail braids off the top of her head, Chrissie Hynde–style bangs hiding her mascara-smudged eyes, blow-job red lips pressed together in an angry line, form-fitting mock Pucci-patterned knit dress (with holes) suffocating her skin, and cracked motorcycle boots jingling as she takes one step after another.

My world comes to a dead halt. I'm Judge Reinhold in *Fast Times at Ridgemont High* and she's Phoebe Cates, a dripping, sultry destiny approaching in slow motion as the Cars' "Moving in Stereo" plays. Her eyes lock with mine, no one exists except for me and her; we're off to change our worlds. Her top lip curls, almost a smile forming on the right side of her mouth; she is assessing me, evaluating me, with those cut-you-like-a-razor blue eyes, and as her neck cranes down, I notice that there is a tattoo of something sinister snaking up the back of it. And here I am, in my hipster blond/red/almost-white streaks peppering my brunette mane, my too tight designer jeans, my sparkly pink sneakers; so unsubtle.

Already I am intimidated.

"Tell me you are not here because of some man," she sneers. She has an accent. It's Australian.

I've come here, to Jalouse Janes in bumfuck Brooklyn, recommended by my dominatrix friend, Whitney, for a bikini wax. "Um, yeah. No, I'm writing an article." I lie, already wanting to please her.

"You better not be, pixie." She doesn't break character, she just stands there, oblivious to the whirlwind of activity surrounding her, assistants barking and patrons awaiting. Will she humiliate me further by predicting the "design" I am seeking? "The fucking *NY Observer* just did a whole article on this shit, calling Brazilian waxes a trend. Fucking Gwyneth Paltrow and Courtney Love." I gulp; I'm quoted in there, tittering about on how a waxed vaj is like having a birthday ribbon on it, screaming out to the private world, *Open me*. "A fucking guy wrote it. As if he gets it." She spins on her heels and clink-clanks down the long, pink-neon-lit, blue-walled corridor. I don't know whether to follow her, to stand there, to walk out.

"She wants you," her assistant, Rolf, whispers in my ear. I'd forgotten about the Midwestern boy with the European name who took my coat when I walked into this body shop.

"Excuse me?"

"She wants you to be her client. Go, silly." He puts his giant palm on the small of my back and shoves me along. "Gooooo. She has another client coming in forty-five minutes."

I go.

I'd gone to the quite famous J Sisters, based on the hype of their Brazilian waxes, the ones where you as an adult woman emerge with a bare-assed little girl's not-a-pube-in-sight pussy, and was less than satisfied by the clinical atmosphere. You know, hot wax, rip hair, hot wax, rip hair. I can tolerate the physical shock of the wax experience, my pain threshold is higher than most people's; I gave birth without a drug in sight, after all. No, the sterility of the J Sisters, the impersonal, don't-look-you-in-the-eye demeanor of the place put me off. I wanted a professional I could be naked with, that would tend to me with a certain sweetness, that would know the details of my life without getting involved, the kind of business affair I had with my masseur, Paul. Someone intimately involved in the nuances of my va-jay-jay (my new favorite euphemism, coined by Dr. Bailey of *Grey's Anatomy*), but not personally so. I didn't want a J Sister who wouldn't remember me from one appointment to the next; I wanted a pussy-in-arms.

I bumped into Whitney rather randomly at an Upper East Side kids' store. She was pregnant, I was on my way to a baby shower but needed a present, and this store was the closest to the woman's home. We traded anecdotes (Whit: "You cannot believe this submissive who came to me last month"); Whitney admired my sleeping baby daughter, smiling in her stationary somnambulance; Whitney lifted her mini skirt ever so slightly to reveal her mons. There it was, a perfectly formed pubic-hair-encrusted whip. "It's brand spanking new."

"That's amazing," I cooed. I touched the still pink but sensually smooth skin of her mound, and traced my finger over the clean line of the whip.

"Isn't it?"

"Who did that?"

"I've found my Jesus. Her name is June. You have to use her." Whitney reached into her spiky latex hobo bag, dropping the loose folds of her skirt, and pulled out her wallet, fishing; then she found it, a card, and handed it to me. June's card.

"Oh yes want this," I said.

"You tell her you're my friend, OK? She'll make your pussy melt." We both laughed at her faux pas, while the stuck-up salesgirl backed away from us.

I called that day.

"Jalouse Janes, this is Rolf," the Midwestern boy with the faux-European accent said.

"Hi, I'd like to make an appointment."

"Yes honey, for what? We do piercings, tattoos, waxes."

"A wax."

"What kind?"

"Um, I don't know. What do you think?"

I could hear the sharp intake of his breath. "Well, the conventional go for Brazilian. But we'll put you in with June. She'll take care of you." We discussed dates and then Rolf said, "And if you have your period, you'll need to reschedule."

So I don't have my period at the moment but what I do have is a case of the butterflies, particularly because I am crushing on this girl. This vision. Who is no longer in my sight line.

I scamper quickly down the pink-neon-lit, blue-walled corridor, frantically looking for the clue, which door the White Rabbit ran through.

"In here," she drawls, as she sees me rushing by.

I back up and then enter her chamber. It's candlelit, sandalwood incense burning, no surprises. The table where I am to lie sits in the middle of it all, the walls are barebones, except for her framed practitioner's license, June, center square, huddled over tiny vats of wax. She speaks without looking at me: "Have you been waxed before?"

Do I tell her I've been to one of the J Sisters? That would take my cred factor completely away, wouldn't it? "Yes, I have," but not wanting to admit anything, I quickly add, "Whitney sent me to you."

"Whit, huh?" June smiles. "I wouldn't take you for a client of Whit's."

"I'm not," I reply. June seems surprised, as if someone like Whitney would deign to speak to someone who wears pink sparkly sneakers. "I've known her awhile."

"Huh. Interesting." June walks over to her stereo and hits play. The drone of Nick Cave's "Into My Arms" fills the room.

"I love Nick Cave."

"Good. He's all I have at the moment. Would you get naked for me?" I would love to, I think. June folds her arms across her chest. She's going to watch me. I stand there, an idiot in headlights. I'm not expecting this, an audience as I undress. I drop my Prada backpack on the floor, kick off my sneakers, and unbutton my pants.

I look up at her, and her gaze is locked on mine. Are we about to enact a porn scene? Is she going to walk over to me and lick my ass as I arch my back, groaning on cue? I feel warm between my legs, and pull my undies down with my pants. If she's going to be my Asia Carrera, I may as well go for it. I stand upright, waiting for her to make her wakka-wakka move, but she doesn't.

"Your top too." She smiles.

"Won't I feel cold?"

"Oh, right." June turns and I quickly take everything else off, and sit on the table, upright and naked. "You can wear this." She hands me a black mohair cardigan. "I knit it." I was expecting one of those paper robes, but whatever.

"OK, let's get to it." She moves between the stirrups and pats the foot holders. "Put 'em up." She sits on her stool and puts on what probably used to be a coal miner's hat, with a little headlight. Man.

"Um, should we talk about . . ."

"Why don't you let me do my job," she says, neither snapping nor cooing, merely ordering, as she inspects my bush. I lay on the crinkly paper-laden waxing settee, listening to Nick Cave, as she touches my pubic hair, occasionally twirling the curlicues just a bit more; I pray my body doesn't betray me, letting her know how turned on I am by her touch. Finally, as if she's arrived at her decision, she looks up, her palm cupping my pleasure zone. "OK, I'm ready. Are you?" My unconventional authority figure doesn't wait for my answer, she turns to fiddle with her tools. Her powders, her waxes, her sticks. "You did the right thing by snipping your hair for me," she remarks.

"How can you tell?" I say before I have a chance to stop myself.

She hovers above me, rolls her eyes at me. "It's a gift," she says sarcastically.

Everything is a blur. I don't flinch, there is not a tear rolling down my face, I don't mind it at all. It's an exquisite pain; I relish in it. At the end, when I look at myself, I see a design. A lightning bolt.

June gives me a cream to keep my mound moisturized. "Come back when you feel like having another go."

"My husband is Aussie," I say, not wanting this session to end.

"You're married?"

"Barely." This is true. My husband is simply a fuck-stick, nothing more, nothing less.

"So you're doing this for . . ." She knows now I'm not writing an article.

"For me. Really." Every so often, when my husband and I are lounging around, he'll take a razor to me, shave me barely, barely shave me, whatever. It's an open door to fucking, which is all we do when we're not being parents. I don't love him, I look forward to the moment when we've exhausted our lust, when we can be released from each other's hold.

"Huh." She looks at me, really looking at me. "You don't seem very happy."

She says this, and I burst into tears. I'm not happy; in fact, I'm beyond unhappy, although I'm not depressed. I'm trapped in a sad, sad void. I don't love the man whose cock fills me, I don't love the man who sleeps beside me, I don't love the man who holds my child gently in his arms. I put up with him, I pay for his food and his wine and his clothes and his rent, and he services my needs, and that's it. He's not my knight, he's not my Keanu, he's not my fantasy; he's just a mistake. June moves to comfort me, and I tell her not to. "I need to do this," I say, and she understands; I need to cry, I need to gut the pain out. I'd wanted happily-ever-after, but I don't have it. I have a marriage I need to end, soon, before I'm destroyed.

June walks over to the phone and whispers into it, "Tell Rolf not to disturb me. We're running a half hour late." I lie back on the table and put my hand over my eyes, sobbing harder than I ever have, harder than when my best friend committed suicide or when the Towers fell three months after that. I can't stop, I can't stop. And I'm still more or less naked. I hear her lock the door, dim the lights further. June comes over to the table where I lie and climbs aboard. Lies on her left side, alongside me. She props her head up on her left arm and traces the outline of her work with her right hand, her talons tickling me. "I'm not happy either," she says.

I look up at her, and with her face inches away from mine, those lips don't seem angry, they seem hungry. Her eyes are no longer empty, but full of intent, passion, empathy. "Thanks," I say. We look into each other's souls, and her right hand strokes my hips, and everything around me feels like it's undulating; we're alone. A serenity engulfs me and I feel safe for the first time in forever.

She places her lips on my forehead, marking her territory. And then she lays her head beside mine. I feel like we're doing a reverse of the Annie Leibovitz–shot *Rolling Stone* cover, with me as an unclad Yoko and her as a fetal-positioned clothed John Lennon. I close my eyes as her right arm pulls our bodies closer, and there we cleave, for an eternity.

Rolfs raps on the door. "June, it's time."

We both snap to attention, having fallen asleep. June sits up, reaches between her legs, and groans, "You've made me wet," and smiles. *I made her wet.* "My client has been sitting out there for a half hour, for me, can you believe these people?" June watches me as I dress, and as I pull on my pants, she says, "I have to go make nice," and leaves without saying anything else. I grudgingly take off her jumper, smelling it one last time; she wears Shalimar, as I do.

I'm blindsided by her hit-and-run; aren't we supposed to exchange numbers? I don't know what the etiquette is. Do I leave her a tip? For the wax or the healing? I can't tell. I decide to scrawl my e-mail address on a piece of paper and shove a few twenties into the small tip envelope sitting on her desk. I jut out, into the blue neon womb of hustle and bustle, but there's no June, only Rolf.

"Well, that must have gone well," Rolf says with a knowing smile.

"Yeah. How much do I owe?"

"That was complimentary, lovey." Rolf stares at me, thinking his naughty thoughts.

So I leave. Walk to the L train, feeling . . . healed. I don't feel heavy, sad; the ache I've felt for the last year seems to have faded away. June melted my weight, not my pussy. She waved a magic wand, and voilà, gone. Just with her body, her sensual, nonsexual, warmth, she fixed what no one's been able to do, not even myself.

Amazing.

My husband is listening to Nick Cave in the bedroom, the baby has fallen asleep in her stroller, I am ringing Jalouse Janes. "Do You Love Me?" Nick is bellowing, a demand. It's a month later, and the phone message barks that Jalouse Janes has closed shop. Up and done closed. No explanation, no forwarding address. I place the phone down and go into the bedroom. I lie beside my husband, who puts his hand between my legs. I'm wet, thinking of June. "You need to go," I tell him, as his lush lips find my neck, and bite, and his two fingers lunge, tickling the spot they own for now. "Yes, you need to go."

Permanent: The Persistence of
Arab Beauty Rituals

MAYSAN HAYDAR

The recipe is simple: equal parts water and sugar (or honey), and a squeeze of lemon juice. Bring the mixture to a boil and then simmer until it browns. Immediately remove from heat and let cool a bit. Pour onto a heat-resistant plastic surface, and allow to cool to a degree where the taffy can hold but is still sticky and pliable. Pull off enough to comfortably fit your palm and massage between your fingertips until the warm candy comes away from your skin easily, but is still tacky.

Push the taffy along the growth on whichever body parts' hair offends you, press down, and rip away in the opposite direction. Repeat until every undesirable hair on your body has disappeared.

It's safe to say that every woman in the Middle East— regardless of class, culture, religion, or whether her country is in conflict—does this process every few weeks; at least every few weeks for years until the follicles give up altogether. The great thing about the simplicity of the recipe is that there is no excuse for laxity in your appearance: Just because you are a Bedouin living in a desert tent, or an urban woman experiencing food rationing in wartime doesn't mean you can't tidy up your body.

There's no primer or official beauty education for Arab women about what's expected of them or what they're to look like. But very early on, little girls who pay attention at parties see how fancy the women in their families look, and want to join in the prettying-up the mothers, older sisters, aunts, and grandmothers have before big events.

Having been born and raised in the United States by Syrian immigrants, I've learned the rules piecemeal. There wasn't much of a community around when I was a child, so congregating with other Arabs was a novelty. But it doesn't take much observation to figure out the beauty strategies of my people; here's a concise list of indispensable pan-Arab beauty standards: hairlessness, kohl, henna, nice skin, and in the appropriate setting, very very colorful, heavy makeup.

Hairlessness is achieved by the method mentioned above, and while it is required of any skin that shows, the assumption is that women are removing everything else as well (perhaps the term *Brazilian wax* should be adjusted). Kohl is applied liberally and not just for accentuating the eyes; Arabs slather it on babies for all the same fabled benefits that carrots promise. Henna is used as a hair dye and to decorate skin with temporary ornate tattoos. As hair dye, it gives dark hair a red tint and turns white or gray hair bright orange-red; for years, I assumed my hair would grow bright red as I got older, just like my grandmothers'.

Arab women prize light, clear skin, and unlike with Americans, do not see tans as a reflection of health. Even those that are not Muslim or wear *hijab* cover their skin to protect their valuable asset. Scrubbing your skin with rough loofahs and what's known as black soap removes layers of dirt you didn't even know you had, revealing new, supple skin underneath.

Makeup celebrates the bigness of facial features; Arabs give no regard to the makeup maxim of if-strong-eyes-then-subtle-lips. The kohl exaggerates large eyes, bright and unnatural shades highlight the fullness of the mouth and the prominence of cheekbones. The usually accompanying large-ish noses are going through a bit of a change. Whereas before they were just a non-issue, women of my twenty-four-to-thirty-five generation are thinning down their noses and lopping off the tips. While our Semitic sisters seemed often to have little say in the matter (their mothers drove them to the plastic surgeon on the stroke of sixteen), the ladies I know are waiting until they are totally independent from their families, not having surgery until their late twenties. Leading the trend are the women on Arab television. Rather than being the touchstone of terrorism, the newscasters of Al Jazeera are instead the harbingers of trends to come; notably, many of them now have very small, well-carved noses.

The most phenomenal difference between Arab and Western beauty standards is the intended audience—while there is an unspoken competition between women in the West for the attention of men, the segregated societies of the Middle East and North Africa (both historically and whatever remnants remain) created an atmosphere in which the women are looking their finest for one another. Orientalists have long fantasized about harems—curvy forms lounging around in opulence, waiting to be called on by male desire. Lady Mary Wortley Montagu painted a sexy picture in her description of the women's bath of the Ottoman Empire—languid, perfumed, and decorated bodies. Appealing girls dancing in beautiful, revealing costumes. The whole harem fantasy exists in real life, with one startling void: There are no men. Nothing about the scene is about seduction or desire: These women are seeking the admiration and approval only of other women, and nothing about it is sexual. Even at events where the sexes commingle, the women will look *nice*, but in a modest, more understated way. There is nothing subtle about the way they dress at ladies-only parties. The aforementioned beauty checklist is immediately obvious. Hair and dress styles ebb and flow with the season (right now, allowing your hair to naturally curl is totally not cool; all the presenters on Arab television have straight, flat hair), but the central process remains the same. Women are getting together to get beautiful to then go to places and be beautiful. The beauty shop in the United States is an almost-there version of this, gay male hairstylists aside. If you are going into an Arab beauty shop to have a trim, set aside the entire afternoon. If you are part of a bridal party, make sure you have the whole day. Every female member of both families is present and washing, waxing, powdering, plucking, moisturizing, making tea, applying, removing, coiffing, curling—manipulating every feature until she's satisfied.

Because of unfortunate current events, Americans get a chance to glimpse Arabian life pretty infrequently. One thing that newspeople have commented on and feminists have lamented is the lack of insight from women. They are notoriously absent from the "Arab street," and we wonder why we don't know what Middle Eastern women think or if they have an opinion at all. The intrepid journalists should perhaps try the beauty parlor. Women have their own places where they congregate, drink tea, and discuss solutions to the region's political problems (or their unmarried daughter's problems, or the neighbor's in-laws' problems—they all seem equally as important).

When I hear about wedding parties being attacked in Baghdad or Amman, it's both a terrifying and yet reassuring reminder of the determination of life. Recent years' turmoil demonstrated one powerful message about culture and beauty rituals: Regardless of conflict, daily life routines continue. Couples are still getting married, and their families are still having weddings. They're still celebrating. Even in a country like Afghanistan, where years ago the fundamentalist Taliban shut down beauty salons, the beauticians moved their businesses into their homes and kept working. The filmmakers behind *The Beauty Academy of Kabul* would have been well suited to visit a salon on the day of a wedding, or attend the wedding itself. While the warmhearted and brave American beauticians' intentions were sweet, their naïveté about their purpose in Afghanistan demonstrates a willful ignorance. The

Americans thought they were rescuing the female population with designer scissors and awards for "testimony [*sic*] to the human spirit." The Afghan students were just looking for useful information—there was no interest on their part for adopting new rituals or styles altogether; put succinctly by Sima, one of the project's expatriate Afghan Americans, they were just looking to learn what chemicals they should not put on their hair. The cluelessness of the American beauticians is made most clear in Terri: She praises her students on how well they were combing hair and she berates the students for their complaints about their Frederic Fekkai scissors. Had the filmmakers attended a wedding, they could have seen why beauty school would be so lucrative. The events are so dressed up, so colorful—it's like the Metropolitan Museum Costume Institute Benefit Gala, the prom, quinceanera, and the Academy Awards—all lumped into one.

The constancy of the events and the rituals that go into them give a sense of comfort during instability, a connection to history, and a sense of community with all women. It's worth the pain of ripping out your hair from the root. Anyway, it doesn't hurt so much after the first couple of times.

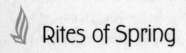 Rites of Spring

SARAH BENNETT

Right before Kelly and I stopped speaking to each other, I went along with her as moral support when she got her first Brazilian wax. The salon was in midtown, not far from where both of her sisters' offices were. We went past the sunny receptionist's desk, through a room of empty massage tables, all the way back to a windowless room with a few chairs and a slurry of women's magazines. We sat there and waited for a door at the other end of the room to open. Kelly would go into that room alone.

Kelly's sisters had joked with her about my presence. "Are you gonna make her hold your hand, Kel?" her sister Lisa had asked. "Just admit you're gay already. I won't tell Mom."

"You're such a bitch," Kelly told her. "You know we're just . . . what did I call it?"

"Platonic life partners," I said.

"When are you going to grow up?" Betsy asked.

Kelly burped.

To Kelly's credit, she was the one with a real job; we met a few years earlier interning at Athlete Records, one of the so-called major indie labels that had an office right above Houston Street. I eventually left due to a lack of upward mobility, a forbidden relationship with a coworker, and the assurance that I could still get free records after my departure. Then I moved to Queens, and as I got through that school year, Kelly and I lost touch.

One night, my roommates threw a party, and while some people came, the turnout was pretty grim, which didn't really shock me. After all, this was Queens. One of my roommates, Martha, had grown up in New York City and had the temperament of someone who was always expecting to get mugged, maybe even hoping for it to happen, because it was her kind of challenge. She had been excited for a certain guy to show up, some friend of a friend who shared her love of the band Tool, and while his goateed, not-Tool-fan friend did make an appearance, the Tool man did not. As I went to bed long after the tepid festivities had wound down, I heard her in her room, sobbing.

"Are you OK?" I asked.

"Go fuck yourself," she replied, sniffling. "I wish you'd move the fuck out."

It's not that I'd never been disliked before, but I'd never been outwardly hated, so I hadn't added it up until then;

the way my two roommates stopped talking when I entered the room, stood up for each other when I asked who had eaten my cereal, laughed at me when I wasn't trying to be funny. When you think about it, you probably haven't been hated either, because hating someone repeatedly, to their face, takes a lot of effort. I lived with two actresses—they had the time to make the effort. All my friends were their friends, which meant I had no friends. So I went upstairs and called Kelly.

That's not the moment we became friends, technically, since that was really months before at Athlete; as easy as it is to pinpoint when Kelly and I stopped being friends, it's much harder to remember when we started. All I know is that when we met, it was through my then boyfriend, Ted, but she didn't know he was my boyfriend at the time, and I didn't know he wouldn't be my boyfriend much longer. Or that my friends wouldn't be my friends much longer. The rules changed every day, and only Kelly seemed able to keep up.

In the months since I left my internship, Kelly got intern-fired and landed an actual record company job, and months after that, after I graduated, I worked in a record store. Her new job had insurance and a 401(k), while, like most of my fellow employees, I got paid under the table and didn't technically work at my store at all. Kelly's sisters, Betsy and Lisa, would sometimes insist on making me dinner or paying for my movie ticket, and I found a way to pay them back in discounts when I could.

When I started interning at Athlete, all my hours then were supervised by Ted in sales, and while Athlete is never lifeless,

I just happened to be there during all the times it was slow. At first, this is all Ted would ever say to me; "It's slow." Then he would stare at the ceiling, or trade a look with JJ the shipping guy, or do busywork in half time. With no one to talk to, I'd just pick one of the three things that he wasn't doing and do it myself. I liked it there, and I loved the free records, so I agreed to stay the whole year.

At the record store, nobody *could* apply for a job because the jobs technically are not and applications don't exist. I'd watch kids stumble in, sheepishly ask the buyer about handing in a CV, and watch him toss it in the trash as the kid left past the security sensors. Somebody tapped me into that job too, but I don't remember who. It seems like I just woke up there one day. Same general business as Athlete, bigger paycheck, different free records.

Ted remained friendly yet monosyllabic right up until I ran into JJ at the falafel place around the corner on a day off. I just nodded to him at first, because I somehow assumed he might have been moonlighting, waiting to pack up some schwarma and send it off with a store order and a bunch of promotional stickers.

"Sarah," JJ said. "It's me."

"Oh, hi! Hey. Going to work?"

"On my break," he said. "You don't work on Tuesdays."

"About to go to class."

He then nodded, very slowly. I waved good-bye as he got a sandwich from the guy behind the counter and backed out, looking at me the whole time. I shook it off and waited in line to place my order. When I got to the front and the guy asked me if it was to go or to stay, it was Ted who answered to stay.

I don't really remember what he said, but not long after we sat down, we were laughing. and I realized that I'd never seen him laughing before and I'd liked it, the way he'd try to hold it in, as if he were using every muscle in his face to clamp down and keep the smile from taking over. Then we were just smiling. Then I looked down at my food.

The pita had split and was oozing hummus blood, and I felt a mild panic; I did not want to eat my sandwich in front of Ted. He seemed too delicate to witness a lunch like this, the way he had such long eyelashes and always seemed to have had tiny cuts on the backs of his hands. When I looked up from my sandwich to Ted's lunch, grape leaves and a spinach pie, so neatly bundled, I thought of the way he sometimes leaned against the back filing cabinet, looked over his desk, and wrapped his arms around himself in a way that seemed more protective than defiant.

Sitting across from Ted, I literally watched him become three-dimensional, like an inflatable toy slowly filling with air. I'd like to think he knew that that would happen, that he didn't need to see me outside of Athlete to understand he had feelings for me, that Ted always understood people the way he understood music, just a little quicker than the rest of the world did. That if Ted saw something in me, maybe the rest of world would too, sooner or later.

Nothing that Kelly did exactly explained why or how she struck me as so funny or cool, especially when we started out, because Kelly was like a good story or a hilarious joke or a major league baseball game; you could try to sum it up in a punch line, but to really understand, you had to be there. Kelly's main gift was making you feel like you were a part of her world just by being there. A world where you got deli guys to happily try to teach you Spanish and where drunk jerks at parties could be convinced you were an eggplant studies major who slept in a nest.

Access to Kelly's world had to be on her terms, though, and her terms were difficult for most to accept; you had to be willing to meet her wherever, whenever, and put up with however many other people she had in her company at that given time. If she called you at four A.M. saying she was in the kitchen of Kate's Joint after closing, running a sundae bar with her friend Anton the delivery boy and a group of kids from Cape Cod she met on the subway, you either put your pants on and went out to meet her or stayed in bed and hoped she might call you again one day down the line.

Also foolish was constantly calling her, praising her, trying to make social plans. She was most wary of those who specifically asked to spend time one on one, or who rolled their eyes when she suggested meeting up with a group. "Whatever, it's cool," she'd say, which, if you knew Kelly, always meant the opposite.

When I got my first call at twelve-forty-five A.M. to meet her, her sisters, and some pro skateboarders she went to high school with at a karaoke place in Chinatown, I didn't think twice. It was better than half sleeping and thinking, *I have made a series of horrible mistakes*. When she and I ended up dueting on some John Denver song and bringing the house to its knees, I'd forgotten the problem altogether.

Months later, once night when she and I were riding junk bikes up and down the Hudson River, I told Kelly about what turned out to be Ted's and my first date at the falafel place. Since it was before the West Side renovation, the piers were still raw, railless slabs of tar and concrete riddled with holes and craters. Sitting in the middle of one with our backs to the city, I felt like I was looking down on the coast of New Jersey from the surface of the moon.

Kelly and I sat there, catching our breath, sharing a carton of fruit juice on our protected island, and the skyscrapers of downtown had our backs, with the umbrella of the Prudential building sheltering us overhead. We talked about what we might want to do if we could avoid the music industry, and if all jobs were as bad as the ones we'd had, and out of nowhere, she asked me what the story was with Ted, anyway. It wasn't until saying it all out loud like a story that I realized it was a full story, and from the past, with a beginning, middle, and end.

"Moment one, dude, shit was off," she said. I just drank the juice. "If he wasn't such an asshole, he would have just asked if you wanted to eat lunch together that first time. It's just passive."

"I don't know if that makes him an asshole."

"You're right," she said. "It makes him a pussy."

He'd been brave at least once; when he first told me he loved me, it was only a few weeks after we started going out. We were on the J train on the way to his neighborhood after work, and after asking me my thoughts on a bunch of Athlete's new releases (I liked, he hated), he just said it.

In retrospect, I understand his angle; he asked me what I thought of some records, and then told me what he thought of me. It shouldn't have been a big deal, but of course it was to me, at least at the time. I smiled but didn't say anything for the rest of the ride, looking out over the bridge, down-river, the lights on either shore seeming warm, orangey and yellow like suburban living rooms. The train labored over the bridge, over the space between the lights, the dark water taking all the warmth from the edges and sweeping it up and away to parts unknown.

Later, Kelly would tell Ted he was a pussy to his face, one night when we were all at the same bar in Seventh Street but had to pretend we weren't. Ted was at the bar with one of his roommates, and Kelly and I were talking in a booth with a bunch of people neither one of us knew but assumed the other one was friends with. We sat and drank and strategized for what seemed like hours, and at one point, when I got up with our pooled funds for another shared drink, Ted made his move and went to talk to Kelly. I know this because I walked back, drink in hand, and saw his face talking to her face, and I realized we were each pretending the other wasn't there so we wouldn't have a moment like this, where the bubbles of our universes touched and our lives starting mixing again, the pair of us as bleach and ammonia, two otherwise inert materials that became toxic when combined.

At first, I just tried to keep myself steady, to keep the drink from spilling, but as I got closer, I saw that Kelly was doing most of the talking, and when I was right behind them, I heard what she had to say.

"I don't see the problem," Ted was saying. "I just want to know if she's mad at me."

"If you care so much, don't be a pussy," Kelly said. "Just fucking ask her. She's in the same room as you right now and you know it."

Ted just shrugged and said nothing. My shoulders sank. I felt liquid drip over the web of my thumb.

"Then you dug your grave, dude," she said. "Get over yourself or get over it, but I've got no more business with you."

Kelly got up and pushed past him to get out of the booth. She saw me, took the drink from my hand, and drank it all in one go.

"If it's all the same to you, let's leave. Do you want to say good-bye to your friends?"

I didn't know what she was talking about; even if I did know those people, even if I knew everyone else in the bar, I knew she was my only real friend in the world. The actresses and college people and high school ghosts were finally gone, and if this was supposed to be the real world, I liked Kelly's version of it.

Whatever she said, on the pier or in the bar, those were the only words that made me feel better about Ted, so I didn't argue. For two years, I never argued with Kelly. Not even at the end.

After Ted, I was single for a while, and Kelly was single for most of the time I knew her too, at least until she met CJ, also known as Claude. Claude was the same height as me, but it always felt like he was peering down on me from a perch, maybe because his head and neck sat atop the mountainous swaddling of clothes that adorned his body, indiscriminate of climate. His jeans were worn low and the fabric puddled above his pristine sneakers. His parka enveloped him like a half-inflated parachute. And his baseball hat always sat on his scalp just so—maybe that's what gave his head the appearance of tilt.

Before I knew Claude, it was Ted of all people who told me he was worthless; before Claude was signed to the record label Kelly ended up working for, his band played a lot of shows on Long Island and made appearances on NYU radio, a place that Ted still had ties to. Kelly liked his stuff—she'd picked up a CD of one of his WNYU performances sold illegally at the store I would later work at, and she would one day be the one to pass that CD of his on to her boss in A&R—but Ted hated it. "Claude's just another Long Island mook with a Cookie Monster voice," he said.

"You don't like it because he's from Long Island?" Kelly asked.

"It's boring," Ted said, shrugging.

"Well, I think it's top-notch," Kelly said. "Gimme back the case. I'm gonna try to contact this guy."

"And say what?" Ted asked.

"That his songs on this CD are rad! Duh!" Then she grabbed the case and wrote some information down while Ted looked at me and rolled his eyes. I looked away.

After work, before Ted and I fell asleep on his miserable futon, he said, "You don't need to be so paranoid at work."

"Huh?"

"You can look me in the eye."

"I wasn't paranoid about Kelly. I just thought you were being mean. It's cool that she's that into something."

"Whatever. She just wants to get into that guy's pants."

Even if Kelly ended up with Claude, I don't think Ted was
right. I'd like to say that, at that moment, he was being an
asshole, but maybe he wasn't.

Kelly swore that her wanting to get waxed had nothing to
do with Claude, and while it might not have been all his influ-
ence, he and her sisters at least shared responsibility for her
decision. "I know you think it's stupid," she said. "You think
everything I do is stupid."

"That's just inaccurate."

Kelly was calling me at the store. I was talking to her away
from the counter in a level, customer voice. I even looked at
stacks of used, to-be-sorted CDs as we spoke, as if I was looking for a title and not a reason for her new aesthetic path.

"You're always on me about the tanning," she said. "And
the nails. I wish you'd stop judging me."

"Only because you're always talking about wanting to
save money," I whispered. "And you always complain how
broke Claude is. You told me you do his laundry at his mom's
house!"

"He buys me dinner when he can, you know that."

"I know, you're the one complaining! And you know I don't
care what you do to your nails. But tanning does give people
cancer. And it is stupid."

"There, you said it!"

"That doesn't make you stupid! Just the thing!"

"Same diff, gotta go."

And then she hung up like someone in a movie, without saying good-bye. I was at work though, so I had to say, "No problem, thanks for calling," to a dial tone.

I imagined Claude, with all of his rare Nikes still in the box, his Japanese toys in the packaging, and his girlfriend, equally pristine, polished, and set away from the rest of the world. At the time, I thought I was supposed to be honest, being a good friend like she had been for me in the bar with Ted, but once someone makes a decision, the window for input is closed. This time, I'd notice the window was there, unlike in Queens, when I walked into the glass and knocked myself out.

When Ted decided just as suddenly that he didn't want to spend time with me anymore, I would have probably put up a fight then if Kelly wasn't around, but I'd already left Athlete and he moved to a new place, so I didn't put in the effort. With Kelly, I always put in the effort. I think this was my biggest mistake.

Two years after graduating from college, I graduated from the record store, and the way you graduate is by getting fired. I was caught giving a discount to Betsy, who was still talking to me, and accused by my supervisor of doing worse. Since I didn't technically work there, however, getting fired didn't have much punch. The store was under scrutiny anyway, after an FBI raid, not for tax evasion but for selling underground hip-hop mix tapes, bootlegged records, and generally unlicensed material. Claude had long since moved on to doing legitimate releases, but I couldn't help but see the irony.

I had gotten too comfortable, so my time at that store, the city's own finishing school for fuckups, had come to an end.

Ted had worked at a similar store before Athlete and left of his own accord, but then again, he didn't really graduate. Last I heard, he's been laid off from Athlete and was working at another record store in Greenpoint.

I remember trying to rationalize that losing my job was just another milestone of adulthood, but since I didn't feel like anything resembling an adult, that didn't make any sense; I had roommates again, I regularly used the word *rad*, and I had recently broken up with my best friend, a girl, a person who had been closer to me and meant more to me than pretty much anyone in the world. I had felt close to men, dated them, had men tell me they loved me and told them I loved them in return, slept with a man's arms around my waist and his nose fit perfectly between two of my vertebrae as if he were trying to share the air from my lungs. Somehow that was not as close as Kelly and me.

It made me wonder how many times one had to come of age before actually getting there, before age was arrived at like the inside of a clean, quiet hotel room after an endlessly delayed flight. I hoped maturity wasn't like success or beauty, one of those things that Claude and Kelly seemed fixated on despite the lack of a fixed goal. Something needed to be attainable for once. It didn't feel like too much to ask.

The clear end of my friendship with Kelly was at a show; I hadn't called her to see if she was going, and she hadn't called me. Since the wax, neither one of us had picked up a phone, but I figured I might see her there. I walked up to the bar, and she was sitting there with her sisters, and Claude, and a few of his friends who were loyal enough to venture outside of

Long Island and their usual social haunts. Our eyes met, but our bubbles never did, just bounced in different directions, up and away.

When Kelly went in to get waxed, I waited on the other side of the thin white door, and all I heard was Kelly's girlish voice asking, "Am I normal? Am I normal?" She asked every couple of minutes, and I had to bite my lip not to laugh. Nobody in the airy front room could hear, none of the phantom patients in the massage room seemed to register it. I thought maybe Kelly and I were communicating telepathically, that we were joking the way we used to. It was almost like the her I used to know was sitting next to me, impatient to leave this stupid place to go see a band, or eat a burrito, or watch movies for ten hours, anything more fun than this. The kind of support Kelly wanted came from the pile of women's magazines next to my chair, but not from me.

When Kelly finally emerged, we made our way up to the front to pay. It wasn't until we got to the sidewalk that I asked her what that was about.

Kelly made a face. "You didn't hear?"

"Hear what?"

"Her! She kept saying, 'So much hair! so much hair!'"

"No way!" I bit my lip again, but it didn't work. I still thought we were both in on the joke.

"Whatever, I'm over it," she said.

"Hey, this lady has seen you *and* your sisters' vages. It's like her and your mom and that's it."

"Do you have a point?"

I stopped in the foot traffic, and midtown business people

streamed all around us. They trampled the last piece of the old Kelly into the sidewalk. "Sorry," I said. "Just trying to cheer you up."

"No point, I'm not upset. You're so weird."

"*I'm* weird! You're the one who—"

"Whatever, it's cool. Can we just go?"

It was strange, in that second, to realize how I knew exactly what she meant without really knowing her anymore at all. I got the message, but I couldn't retreat to my room and call Kelly this time for help. I would never find another Kelly. I didn't really know where I was going to go, where I could find shelter from age coming once again, touching down on my life and flattening the landscape to rubble.

We walked to the subway, the F train at Forty-second Street, and Bryant Park was green and all the tables were filled with couples, families and friends enjoying the May afternoon. The lions outside the public library seemed as noble and eternal as the sphinx in Egypt, and the view up and down Fifth Avenue seemed to go both directions into infinity. Taking it in made me feel lucky, though, and oddly calm, like a warm bed would, or the moment of catching your breath after laughing for a long time, or being in love.

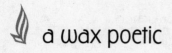 a wax poetic

SARAH JONES

a multicultural affair
this trim trimming party
she speaks mandarin and cantonese
I would speak english french or spanglish
were I not sworn to a vow of stoicism
(silent and dignified, even prostrate and naked
this an african american thing)
my breathing is prana from india
her technique, once brazilian, now a citizen of the world

from waist down I am a brown
brooklyn bagel with a schmear
a flick of the wax
a twist of her tongue depressor
(would that it were only my tongue being

spread thick then tugged clean)
she hovers, coats, yanks, with swiss precision
and soon I am smooth as a saharan dune

in hong kong she was educated as a teacher
she speaks of the rising cost of education
her few days off and how america grinds bones to make
   its bread
at bryn mawr I was educated to be a feminist
to be a torch and find my sexiness where it was buried,
hidden in plain insight
we never speak of how we both got here
or pause to ponder the private, pubic filigree
the tiny pile upon the sterile floor
we do not interrogate the sticky strips
the traps for tortured tufts and tangles

it would be unseemly to tease
apart the reasons some women must touch
other women's pussies every day and
so instead we leave it to the wax
in the melting pot

List of Contributors

Jennifer Belle is the author of the critically acclaimed, widely translated novels *Going Down* (for which she was named best debut novelist of the year by *Entertainment Weekly*) and *High Maintenance* (a national bestseller). Her stories and essays have appeared in *The New York Times Magazine*, *The Independent Magazine* (London), *The New York Observer*, *Harper's Bazaar*, *Ms.*, and *Black Book*. She lives in Greenwich Village, where she leads writing workshops and is developing a television comedy for the FOX network. Her new novel, *Little Stalker*, was published by Riverhead Books in May 2007.

Sarah Bennett's memorial photo hangs at the bar Welcome to the Johnson's on Rivington Street. She is not dead. Find more of her writing at www.ihateselfpromotion.com and www.dateXedge.com.

Francesca Lia Block is the award-winning author of many books of fiction and non-fiction. She lives in Los Angeles.

Julie Burchill has been a writer for thirty years since the age of seventeen. Her latest triumph was the TV adaptation of her young adult novel, 'Sugar Rush,' which won a Stonewall award and International Emmy. She is currently working on her follow-up, *Sweet*. She hopes to become a full-time voluntary worker and theology student by the age of fifty.

Minnie Driver is the Oscar-nominated star of *Good Will Hunting*, *Circle of Friends*, *Grosse Point Blank*, and the FX drama series *The Riches*. She is also a singer-songwriter, whose solo debut, "Everything I've Got In My Pocket," was released last year on Rounder Records.

Samantha Dunn is the author of *Failing Paris* and the memoirs *Not By Accident: Reconstructing a Careless Life* and *Faith in Carlos Gomez: a Memoir of Salsa, Sex and Salvation*. Her work is anthologized in a number of places, including the short story anthology *Women on the Edge: Writing from Los Angeles* (Toby Press), which Dunn co-edited. She is married to musician Jimmy Camp and lives in southern California.

Barbara Ellen is a columnist for the *London Observer* and lives with her two children in London. She is currently working on her first novel.

Susie Essman is a veteran of the world of standup comedy, logging thousands of performances on the Gotham comedy circuit. She has appeared in her own half-hour HBO comedy special, hosted the American Comedy Awards, and performed on *Politically Incorrect* and *Late Night with Conan O'Brien*. She is best known as the foul-mouthed Susie Greene of HBO's *Curb Your Enthusiasm*, now filming its sixth season.

Emma Forrest is the author of the novels *Namedropper*, *Thin Skin*, and *Cherries in the Snow*. She began her writing career as a journalist at age sixteen. Her stories have appeared in *The Sunday Times, The Independent, The Guardian, McSweeney's, Vogue* and *Vanity Fair.* You can visit her website at www.emmaforrest.com.

Judy Forrest has written songs, magazine articles, commercials, and television plays. Her second greatest claim to fame is that her Fig Newtons jingle was sung by Homer on an episode of *The Simpsons.* Her first is that her daughter edited this anthology.

Barbara Hall is a writer/producer for television. She developed *Judging Amy* and created the Emmy-nominated *Joan of Arcadia.* She is the author of seven novels and founder of a band called The Enablers, whose music is available at www.handsome-music.com. She lives in Santa Monica, California.

Maysan Haydar grew up in Flint, Michigan, and Riyadh, Saudi Arabia. Her writing and editing skills were shaped at several magazines, among them *The Nation, Spin, Martha Stewart Living* and *Venus Zine.* She also contributed to *Body Outlaws: Rewriting the Rules of Beauty and Body Image* (Seal Press).

Sarah Jones is the Tony Award-winning writer/star of the one-woman Broadway show *Bridge and Tunnel*, which was produced by Meryl Streep.

Marcelle Karp is the co-founder of *Bust* magazine, the co-author of *The Bust Guide to the New Girl Order* and the author of *Housewife Confidential.* She is happily raising her daughter, Ruby, on her own in New York City.

Ellen Karsh has taught teenagers with disabilities, written grants for the public schools, and headed New York City's grants office under Mayors Giuliani and Bloomberg. She lives in Manhattan and is the co-author of *The Only Grant-Writing Book You'll Ever Need*.

Marian Keyes is the bestselling author of *Angels* and *Sushi for Beginners*.

Lena Levin is a pseudonym.

Rose McGowan, of the long-running series *Charmed*, stars this year in Robert Rodriguez's *Planet Terror* and Quentin Tarantino's *Death Proof*. She is the proud dogmother of Bug and Fester.

Suzanne Moore is an award-winning writer and journalist who lives in London. She has been a columnist for *The Guardian* and *The Independent* and is currently at the *Mail* on Sunday. She has had two books of collected journalism published. She has three children. She doesn't have hay fever.

Helen Oyeyemi was born in Nigeria in 1984 and moved to London when she was four. She is the author of the highly acclaimed novel *The Icarus Girl*, which she wrote while she was still at school, and two plays, *Juniper's Whitening* and *Victimese*. Her second novel, *The Opposite House*, was published by Bloomsbury in May 2007 and by Nan A Talese/Doubleday in June 2007.

Maggie Paley is the author of *Bad Manners,* a novel; *In One Door,* a play about Edith Wharton; *Elephant,* a chapbook of sestinas; and a non-fiction book, *The Book of the Penis,* which has been translated into twelve languages. She's published articles in *Vogue, Elle, Mirabella, O,* and a host of other magazines, and reviews in *The New York Times Book Review* and *Bookforum*. She lives and works in New York.

Rachel Resnick is the author of the *LA Times* bestselling novel, *Go West Young F*cked Up Chick*. Her work has also appeared in *Tin House, Blackbook,* the *LA Times,* and *LA Weekly.* Her website is www.RachelResnick.com.

Laren Stover has published three books: a novel, *Pluto, Animal Lover,* a finalist for the Discover Great New Writers Award; *The Bombshell Manual of Style;* and *Bohemian Manifesto: A Field Guide to Living on the Edge.* She has written essays for *The New York Observer, The New York Times, Mr. Beller's Neighborhood,* and *German Vogue;* plays; short stories; and a libretto for a song cycle, *Appalachian Liebesleider,* which premiered at Carnegie Hall. She is a fellow of Yaddo and Hawthornden, and a recipient of The Ludwig Vogelstein Foundation Grant for fiction and the Dana Award.

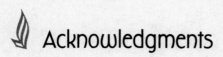 Acknowledgments

I am grateful to my intern, Kathleen Comfort, for her transcription of interview tapes.

Copyright Notices